OBÍ

Oracle of
Cuban Santería

For my god-sister, Carrie Mikel, and for my godfather, John Pilato.
Both deserve more than just a book dedicated in their names.

OBÍ

Oracle of

Cuban Santería

Ócha'ni Lele

Destiny Books
Rochester, Vermont

Destiny Books
One Park Street
Rochester, Vermont 05767
www.InnerTraditions.com

Destiny Books is a division of Inner Traditions International

Library of Congress Cataloging-in-Publication Data

Lele, Ócha'ni
    Obí—oracle of Cuban Santería / Ócha'ni Lele
    p. cm.
    Includes bibliographical references and index.
    ISBN 0-89289-864-6
    1. Orishas—Cuba. 2. Santería—Cuba. 3. Divination—Cuba.   I.
Title: Ócha'ni Lele. II. Title.
    BL2530.C9 M94 2001
    299'.64—dc21
                                    2001002677

Printed and bound in the United States

10 9 8 7 6 5 4 3 2 1

Text design and layout by Priscilla Baker
This book was typeset in Stone Serif, with Greymantle and Bodega Sans as display faces

Contents

Acknowledgments

WHEN A WORK OF THIS SCOPE is being written, no one author can claim credit for all its contents. The words are mine; the work is mine; the interpretations are mine. This book represents countless hours of writing, rewriting, worry, and sweat. Yet Santería is an oral faith, and its true secrets are not to be found in the myriad volumes already on the market; its mysteries are found in the hearts and souls of those who practice this religion.

For this book, I am in great debt to my godfather, Eshu'leri Bolafun (John Pilato), for his patience and thorough instruction. He teaches not with the mouth but with his heart, and his love for this religion is reflected in all that he does. To Naomi Alejandro, Christine Jaffe, Michael Cabrera, Akin Babatunde, Ogúndei (Evaristo Peréz), and many others, I am in debt for my own vast knowledge of ebó.

My publisher, Inner Traditions, cannot go without acknowledgment; I must thank Jon Graham and Laura Schlivek for their countless hours of hard work as they turned this manuscript (and my previous work) from a dream into reality. My former copy editor, Susannah Noel, was a tireless tyrant (said in love, of course) when it came to polishing my previous book, *The Secrets of Afro-Cuban Divination*. I learned so much by working with her; how can I thank her for pushing me, and my writing skills, to the limit?

Doris Troy, the copy editor for this book, was just as thorough, and gave *Obí: Oracle of Cuban Santería* the final bit of polish it needed to become the masterpiece it is. Thank you Doris! Finally, I would not be in this religion at all except for Oyá, who claims and guides my head in life; if I owe anything to anyone, I owe all to her. She has given me a life where I thought I had none, and there is no greater gift than that. Aché to you all.

Introduction
Beyond the Middle Passage

When my head is on my shoulders,
my feet in salty waters, and my thoughts extend
beyond the horizon, there is no doubt in my mind
that I stand facing the ocean.
—A proverb from the diloggún, babá Eji Ogbe

STANDING ON THE ATLANTIC SHORE and gazing at the ocean's endless surf, I know peace and fear. There are no other words to describe the feelings that Olokun, the bitter sea, evokes. I stand at the crest of land and sea, where waves roll relentlessly against the coastline, hungrily sucking sand to sea before churning it once more against the shore. I am still as she laps at my feet. The tide is receding slowly, yet the waves are ceaseless and the sand moves constantly. My footing dissolves; I shift my weight back and to the side to keep my balance. Blocking the morning sun with cupped palms, my eyes follow the path of bubbling sunlight over the water and into the horizon; it ends in the blue ocean and the bluer sky, into a gentle, sloping curve that slips from view. I am lost in this moment, lost with the sand amid foaming waves. Eternity lives here, in the ocean, and it is to this place that I come, again and again, to rest, to meditate, to cleanse, to recharge. I yearn to mingle with the natural forces as they, too, merge and mingle with each other.

Today I have not come alone; my godmother, Jackye, and her friend Josephine have brought me. Both are *santeras,* priestesses of an Afro-Cuban faith known as Santería, a religion that survived more than four hundred years of slavery and persecution by white and Hispanic slave lords. It is a spirituality that nourished the souls of those oppressed for no reason other than the silky blackness of their skins. Torn from their homelands, sold and bought like chattel, raped, abused, beaten, and packed into the filthy cargo bays of slave-trading ships, the followers of the *orishas* (spirits) came to the New World with no more than the *aché,* the power, of the orishas within their heads. Those who had time swallowed the sacred shells of their gods, taking their physical forms on earth into their bodies; thus were they able to hide their spirits from their captors. Inevitably, these relics passed through their bodies; once again they swallowed them and held them secretly in their bellies. For months priests and priestesses suffered in darkness, bound in iron chains as seamen guided the marine prisons over the ocean. Some mortally mangled themselves to escape these bonds, finding release and peace only as they flung themselves over the ship's bow, consigning their lives into the ocean's icy grip, Olokun's womb. The rest suffered agonizing pain and torment, praying to her for strength, for release, for safe passage.

Of the hundreds of blacks crammed into cramped quarters, only a few survived each crossing: the determined, the strong, the devoted. Those who died were tossed overboard by the ship's crew without care or concern, left to sink to the cold, salty depths. Yet the same qualities that enabled those few to endure also enabled the orishas to survive. Priests of the white Christ tried in vain to convert the African souls. Although they had neither the morals nor the strength to destroy the sin of slavery, they assuaged their own festering guilt by baptizing blacks "in the name of Jesus." But while the slave masters could coerce the bodies of their servants, they could not conquer their Yoruba spirit. The holy saints, say some, looked down in pity and despair at what their own people were doing; and the orishas, in their infinite wisdom, carried the followers through the hardships of slavery. In secret, in hiding, disguising their gods behind the willing masks of the saints, priestesses and priests of the orishas continued to nourish the spirits, and the orishas, in return, sustained their followers through the centuries, helping them to evolve, to grow in a prison that was not of their making, in a world that they did not want.

History is a fragile cloth, its threads easily broken, its patterns dulled by the past that created it. Nature is cruel, destroying what she has wrought with her own hands. Time, even time devours his own children. The cries of our ancestors, however, still echo in the angry, crashing waves. We can hear them, and remember, if we listen. We must listen.

It has been more than four centuries since the first slaves were brought to the New World, and although slavery has been abolished, their descendants are still oppressed by a society that disapproves of not only their skin color, but also their native spirituality. I stand with my elders at the ocean's edge, the end of the Middle Passage. My godmother, Jackye, is a priestess of Obatalá, mother and father to the earth, the great ruler of the heights sent forth by Olódumare to create upon the watery void. Josephine, an elder, a Puerto Rican santera, is a priestess of Yemayá, the orisha brought forth from Olokun's depths as Obatalá chained her from land. Unable to resist the supreme deity's sanctions, yet too vast to be restrained by Obatalá's chains, Yemayá was born from Olokun's prison; she became the owner of the ocean's waves and of all the fresh water upon the earth. We had come to honor this mighty goddess, the world's queen. Josephine and Jackye had brought an array of offerings: watermelons, pork rinds, and dark molasses—delicacies of the orisha.

Unknown to them, I had brought my hopes and my fears. I am white and entering an African religion; and although my godmother herself is white, I could not help but wonder if I really belonged in such a faith. Before the sea I suddenly became frightened. I could imagine the souls of the ancestors out there, embraced in Olokun's icy grip. I could imagine their pain, their terror, as they were flung carelessly into a watery abyss. I was in awe of them, of the ocean's vast depths, of its strengths and powers. Shaking, I stepped back from the water.

"Bonito," Josephine questioned, using her pet name for me, "what is wrong? Why do you shake?"

Quietly, so Jackye could not hear, I told the elder my thoughts, my fears. She laughed. "I am not black either, Bonito; I am Spanish. Let me tell you a story about how the orishas came to this place and how they came to be worshiped by all peoples," she said as we both sat down on the hot sand.

Many centuries ago, so my own godmother told me, the orishas lived only in Africa, the cradle of civilization and the mother of all our races. Yet came the Spanish, the whites, to the holy continent, and with them they brought the evils of a modern world. Many of our priests and priestesses in old Oyó became corrupt when they saw the wealth that these men brought, and they were told that they could exchange the symbols of their orishas, the diloggún, *for the wealth of gold. "We can wash our spirits anew," they rationalized, "and have the wealth that these strange men bring, for surely this is the will of our gods." In ignorance, they went to the ships and lay down their sacred implements for the precious metals that the traders carried; yet instead of receiving gold coins as they had been promised, they were given iron shackles and taken prisoner over the sea. No one heard from them again. Then the slave lords returned once more, and this time they offered the village chiefs gold in exchange for the strongest and healthiest of their people. These, too, were forced into submission and taken away over the bitter seas. Finally, having weakened the tribes through their own greed and sin, the traders returned once more and uprooted what they could of the empires, using their weapons of war to force into submission those who were unable to run. Thus did the evil of slavery begin with greed and lies, and thus did it continue over the centuries.*

Many of the orishas came with their priests, secreted either in their hair or in their bellies. Some who could sailed through their elements:

Obatalá in the sky, Shangó in the storm, Aganyú in the volcano. Others were already there, in Cuba: Orúnmila and Elegguá, who are everywhere and know everything, and Ogún, who rests deep in the earth wherever there is iron. Yet one orisha could not leave. Oshún, who lived in the sweet river waters of Africa, tried in vain to follow her people over the ocean. Yet she could not, for when the river meets the seas, the fresh waters become salty, and therein she could not travel. So she went to her sister Yemayá and called her, begging, "Sister, where do my people go? Why can I not follow?" And tears slowly slid down her face, tears of sadness and anger.

"Sister," said Yemayá, "our people are being stolen away to a place called Cuba, and those of us who are able are going with them in spirit to watch over them, to protect them as best we can. Some of us are already there, for our realms extend to theirs. Others are carried in the bodies of the priests and priestesses, for their faith in us is great. Yet you, Sister, cannot go. Your followers have traded their diloggún for iron out of greed for gold, and your river ends at the sea. I am sorry."

Yet Oshún knew that her sister Yemayá was very powerful, being the mother of all the orishas. And she knew that if she truly asked, her sister would find a way to carry her across the seas. "Sister, I am sad; I am angry. Yet I forgive those who have brought this evil. I forgive those who have acted in greed. I want to be with them, to protect them, to make their lives sweet. How can I go to Cuba?"

Yemayá thought for a moment, then smiled. "You are fresh water nourished by my rain. You will travel with me to Cuba through the sky, in the rain with your lover, Shangó, and with the blessings of our elder Obatalá."

Again Oshún shed tears, this time of joy, and she asked, "Sister, what do the people in Cuba look like? Are they like us with dark skin and curly hair?"

"No, Sister, they are lighter. Some are brown and others are white. They do not look like us."

"I have another wish, my sister. I want to look not only like our people but also like theirs. I want to show all those the beauty of the orishas and the evil that they have wrought on our people. I want to *show them all that life can be sweet, that there can be harmony, that there can be love. I want to show all who will adore us the gifts of Oshún."*

Yemayá smiled as she straightened Oshún's hair and lightened her skin; she became the most beautiful of mulattoes, yet retained her African features. She was voluptuous, stunning. "This is only illusion, my sister. Those who look upon your beauty will see those things that they find most beautiful—through you they will learn that no matter the hardships, the bitterness in life, it can be sweet if they honor you and what you represent: love for all peoples and love for the orishas." With those words, Yemayá took Oshún into herself, into the rain, and together they traveled to Cuba to watch over the Yoruba race. Yemayá was their mother and helped them to adapt, to survive, to grow, while Oshún taught that despite the bitterness in their lives, there could be sweetness. Thus did all the orishas finally come here to the New World—and thus have they been worshiped by all.*

Josephine gently nudged me. "The orishas are black; we worship the black gods of black peoples, and still they love us as we love and honor them. Yet their love does not come without a price. There are those who would call our practices barbaric, pagan, primitive. Much of our religion is outlawed, and even now there are those fighting the wars of persecution and spiritual enslavement in courts of 'justice.' Have you not heard of the *iyawós* [initiates] going to jail, arrested on the throne during what is the greatest moment of their lives? To honor the gods that we love, we must sneak, at times, in shadows or risk imprisonment for our beliefs. We must suffer still at the hands of Catholics and Christians who taunt us with their holy books, saying ours are the ways of Satan. We watch as our brothers, sisters, and elders come from Cuba and

---

* This *patakís* (legend) is not native to Africa; no one in Nigeria who practices native Yoruba religion is familiar with it. It is a story designed to illustrate the universal principles of the orishas, and how the religion of the Lucumí came to be practiced by those peoples beyond the original Yoruba tribes.

are stripped of their holy orishas by customs officials who hope to rid our 'evil' from the earth. Although it is not slavery, although the hardship does not match that of our ancestors, we still suffer. Yet we all work hard for the day when we may once again come out into the open, when blacks may reclaim in pride and without prejudice the orishas of their ancestors, and we may work with them side by side, healing the wounds of the past. We suffer for their love, yet Oshún makes our suffering sweet. She is truly the most beautiful of the orishas. But I ramble, and it is time to make our offerings to Yemayá, our mother."

Josephine motioned for Jackye bring the basket with the ocean's offerings. Standing between us, Josephine began to chant, to pray in the ancient tongue known as Lucumí. Jackye and I held her hands, for she was becoming unsteady, dizzy, as she communed with the natural forces of her mother orisha. The litany became interspersed with Spanish. I could pick out bits of prayers for my godmother, for me, wishes for both our physical and our spiritual health. She called on the strength of the ancestors and said blessings for their elevation and for our protection. It was time to make an offering. We threw whole melons into the ocean; I swung Josephine's hard and watched as it landed only a few feet away, rolling and bobbing in foamy waves. Josephine threw handfuls of pork rinds to her mother, while Jackye let molasses pour freely into the churning foam. Children came running along the shoreline, puzzled, as grown-ups were throwing food into the water. "Little Elegguás," Josephine said, tilting her head toward them in acknowledgment.

Helping Josephine back to our chairs on the beach, I strained to listen over the crashing waves. They rumbled and thundered, stirred up by the invocations and prayers Josephine had intoned, as my own godmother began her string of prayers with fresh water to Elegguá, opener of roads and messenger to the orishas, to the sea, to Yemayá. In her hands were rounded slices of coconut meat, and as she prayed she threw slivers into the waters. Clapping her hands, she let the pieces fall, chanting to herself once more as she poured the last of her molasses into the cresting waves; again, she picked up the pieces of coconut and threw them to the ground with a swift flick of her wrists. "*Ejife,*" she yelled over the roaring waves. "The world is in balance." Yemayá was pleased with her offerings. Slowly, Jackye knelt down to the sand to retrieve the coconut for one last question; an errant wave crashed onto the beach, spraying her with its mist. By instinct, she turned her head as cold water ran over her back. Turning again to retrieve the four pieces, Jackye's hand touched only sand.

Yemayá had accepted her offerings; Yemayá would say no more!

ONE
Understanding the Orisha Obí

AMONG THE YORUBA, there is a basic system of divination known as Obí. It is an oracle cut anew for each use from the seeds of the kola tree *(Cola acuminata),* a tropical species prolific on the continent of Africa. The Yoruba believe that each seed is sacred, symbolic of the earth, cosmos, and Olódumare. A perfect ripe seed yields four lobes when split. Two of the lobes are called *obí,* and it is from these portions that the oracle is named. These lobes are feminine in shape, being rounded and bulbous at one end; the other two lobes are phallic, oblong. These are considered the masculine portions and are known as *akó.* Unbroken, one seed is a creative synthesis, a fusion of the masculine and feminine halves of nature, a perfect union holding the potential for new creation. As the orisha devotee rips open the flesh, his own world is symbolically torn asunder, and only under the direction of his patron orisha will this world be rebuilt. After a solemn prayer and a heartfelt invocation to the spirits, a random toss of these four pieces is directed by unseen hands. Thus is the orisha's will revealed.

Mathematically, four separate pieces of anything yields only five patterns, yet separating the four lobes into two divisions, masculine and feminine, increases the number of "letters" that can open into a total of ten. And with the numerous ways in which the lobes can fall upon each other, a limitless number of signs is created. By these the initiated can determine the orisha's desires. The basic patterns that fall in the Kola-nut oracle have names: *odí, alafia, obita, akita, yeye, ailashara, ejire, ayé, oyekun,* and *iyala.* Respectively, each pattern brings impediments, coolness, blessings, unhappiness, victory, debility, friendship, money, hardship, and health. Beyond these basic patterns, and the patterns within the patterns, the African initiate has the *aché* (power, grace, life, initiation) in his head to divine the full meaning of the mandala that unfolds. The orisha displays his or her letters in Obí before the shrine, but the diviner is allowed to interpret according to his own knowledge and experience. An objective sign (the letter of the oracle) is matched by the subjective knowledge of the priest, and from these two are the spirit's prognostications determined.

When the Catholic and Christian heresies of slavery brought orisha initiates to the New World in hordes, the religion was forced to undergo evolutionary changes. In the areas that later became known as the United States, slavery was so harsh, so brutal, that the orisha traditions could not survive beyond the first generation. Heartlessly, whites divided the family and social units. Mothers and fathers were ripped from each other and from their children, whole families destroyed as the cruel masters sought to push their slaves into submission. Blacks were regarded as animals and tortured to obey, to work, to produce for a race too lazy to produce on its own. Here, among colonies that were first established for "religious freedom," the native religions of Africans died. There was no evolution for the spirits or their followers; there was only cruelty and death.

It seems a paradox, but slavery among the Hispanic, Portuguese, and predominantly Catholic countries was kinder. Although they still were treated as beasts of burden, the Africans' social units were kept intact. Some were even given free, private time to themselves, and it is among these people that the religion survived. Due to a milder climate, many of the herbs used in the orishas' rituals were no longer available; through divination, however, suitable substitutions were found. Those who toiled in the Spaniards' fields still had the initiation and the aché to divine using obí; however, the oracle's kola nut was no longer in plentiful supply. Through divination, another substitute was sought. Some say that it was Obatalá who sanctioned the change; others say nothing less than a decree from Olófin himself could change the methodology of the religion. No matter to which orisha the new system is credited, the divination system was adapted. Instead of a four-lobed nut, the coconut (which also exists in Africa) became the oracle. The new tool was named Obí divination as well, yet it had for its patron a different obscure orisha of the Yoruba pantheon, Obí, from whom the coconut was created. It is this system of divination and myth that continues to flourish throughout Cuba and the rest of the New World.*

The Myth of Obí, the Sacred Coconut

(This myth originates in Obara Osá, pattern 6–9, in the diloggún.) Of all Obatalá's mortal creations, Obí was perfect, pure. Born with all heaven's blessings, his life was one of charity and servitude. Surrounded by poverty, he would surrender his wealth to support the needy—beggars and vagrants were his friends. In the midst of despair, his was the voice that could soothe. Obí's words were kind, and never uttered in vain. Such was the beauty within the man that it formed his body in its image. The mortal's skin was polished, smooth like onyx; his eyes, dark like pools of ink, reflected all around him. No woman's skin was softer, yet no man's form

---

* Unlike the native Yoruba form of obí divination, the New World form is named after an actual orisha, Obí. It is believed that the orisha himself is embodied in each single coconut; therefore, when referring to Obí divination in the diaspora the name is capitalized, as the orisha and the coconut are one and the same.

more masculine. Obí's body was solid, chiseled, and toned, yet when he walked its suppleness was sensual and rhythmic, like music. So devoid of vanity and evil was Obí that Olófin favored him, granting him eternal life. The beauty that was within Obí shone greater than that without, and by his aché Olófin made it gather. Obí glistened with whiteness and purity. All of the orishas agreed that there was none more radiant, more handsome than he.

Others who were born after the creation of humans knew Obí as the coconut, a fruit that once was a brilliant, glistening white. His skin was smooth like marble, yet iridescent like virgin snow; always, his robes were immaculately clean and pressed, reflecting the dazzling light of both sun and moon. Only the robes of Obatalá were kept cleaner. For Obí to walk during the day was to blind the sight of those about him, and all the orishas marveled at his magnificence.

Although elevated for his humility and reverence, Obí's ego grew slowly over the centuries until he believed there was no one more blessed, more important than he. "If beauty is a gift from Olódumare," Obí mused, "then I am the most gifted. Surely it is because of the good works I did on earth. There is none more deserving than I of beauty and eloquence."

Elegguá, who knows all things, knew the darkness that was growing like a cancer in Obí's heart. Many times he warned Obatalá, yet when Obatalá looked at the elevated mortal, he saw only the perfection in his creation. Elegguá went to Olófin, but Olófin was still blinded by the magic he had woven when elevating Obí to the status of an orisha. His aché brought the inner light of the man without; his beauty was enhanced by the whiteness of creation, and even god on earth could not see beyond that. Like many, Olófin mistook physical beauty for spiritual purity. And that purity had been tainted.

Eventually it came to pass that Olófin threw a festival for all the orishas in his own opulent palace. Obí spent many weeks preparing for the party, ordering new robes to be made in the finest white cloths with sparkling white laces and satins. Only the purest fabrics were used, and they were stitched by those with the cleanest hands. When finished, the white clothing contrasted deeply with his dark skin. The power of his aura magnified the whiteness, and together they glistened and scintillated so it seemed Obí himself was the source of all light, that all else was but a reflection of him. He was pleased. The day of the party arrived, and Obí went, assured that there was no orisha better dressed or more magnificent than he.

Arriving early, Obí watched from a distance as the other orishas came: Yemayá in her dress of foam and shells, dripping with pearls and gemstones from the sea; Oshún in her most gorgeous yellow satins; and Shangó in his flaming red trousers and pressed white shirt. Although all had prepared many days for the festival, the clothing of none could compare to what Obí wore. It seemed that he had gathered all that was cool and white in the world, weaving it into a tapestry that shimmered and glistened in the moon's own pale glow. Passing the front gates of Olófin's palace, casting a brilliance almost unmatched by Olófin's splendid walls, Obí saw that a group of ragged, dirty mendicants had gathered by the palace entrance to beg alms from the mighty ones. Their clothing was filthy, caked with mud and dried leaves; the rags they wore were unfit even for an animal, and Obí cringed as he drew closer to them. Gone were his mortal days when he worked selflessly for others; now he was an orisha, and deserving of respect! The vagrants begged for money, and Obí pretended he was deaf. One reached out to touch him, leaving a tiny stain on his whites, and Obí was enraged. "Leave me alone," he said, seething, through clenched teeth. "You do not belong at Olófin's palace; you belong in the forest with animals!" Such was his rage that the magical clothing he wore flared about his figure wildly, whipping in the air as he shook his fists in fury. Stunned, the vagrants could do nothing but shrink from the orisha's outburst, and in fear they ran.

So loudly had Obí roared these words that Olófin himself crept cautiously to the front door to investigate the commotion. He watched sadly as the once humble orisha sent away the poor who had gathered outside the palace. When the last vagrant had disappeared from sight, Olófin looked at his son with pity. He remembered the warnings of Elegguá, that his elevated mortal had become shallow and severe, and his only words were, "Come inside. Join the party." Turning away with sadness in his eyes, Olófin said not another word to Obí that night. He only watched as the orisha mingled among the guests, laughing, eating, and drinking as if he had not a care in the world.

Obí spent the next day analyzing the events. He decided to plan a festival more extravagant than Olófin's, one that would show himself to be the most gracious of all Olófin's children. He hand-picked the guest list, inviting only the most important spirits, including Olófin, father of them all. Word was also sent out—beggars and vagrants were forbidden at his door. Weeks of preparation followed as Obí drove his servants to make his mansion the cleanest, whitest, and most elegant of all dwellings. He forced his tailors and seamstresses to weave the most stunning fabrics from the whitest wools and cottons, adding his own aché into the clothing created. On the night of the party, despite his preparations, only a few of those whom Obí had invited appeared. Attending from curiosity rather than sincerity, the guests exchanged furtive glances and whispered conversation. Obí was furious, for beyond Olófin himself there was no one more grand than he. How dare the others not show up! How dare those in attendance display their ingratitude by whispering, by snickering, by questioning his motives. The hours crawled by. Anger turned to rage, and Obí became the most ungracious of hosts. Later that night, as the orishas were beginning to leave, there was a quiet knock at the door. Obí was still hoping for late arrivals and he ran to answer it.

Rage then turned to fury, for it was just a ragged beggar. His hair was matted and his clothing torn and filthy, and as Obí stared in horror, he held out his hands to beg for alms. The orisha could only tremble as he saw the bleached white walkway to his palace tracked with dirt and mud from the vagrant's feet. Fury exploded.

"How dare you, you dirty, filthy man," Obí thundered. "How dare you come to my house tracking filth, dressed in rags and stinking like a dirty beast! Get away from me and leave this house. I never wish to see you again." Slamming the door in the beggar's face, Obí turned to see all the orishas gathered behind him, their expressions blank in disbelief. A few of them trembled in either fear or rage—Obí could not tell, nor did he care. "Have you gone mad?" asked Elegguá, the first to recover. "How can you call our father a filthy, dirty animal?"

Before Obí could calm himself and question Elegguá, there came yet another knock at the door. Tearing it open, Obí was again enraged as the old man stood before him. As he opened his mouth to scream, the figure began to change and melt until the beggar was no more, and Obí could see what the other orishas saw—Olófin himself. Obí had turned away the true lord of the universe.

The mighty one let show all his brilliance and goodness. The room was basked in white light that blanketed the ivory walls of Obí's mansion; all were blinded in its splendor. The orishas lay down in *foribale* (prostrate salute) before this mighty display of aché, while Obí could only shake and tremble as he sank to his knees to beg forgiveness. Yet no words came, for his tongue loosened and fell from his mouth. Obí was permanently silenced. Rage melted into fear, and fear became desperation as Obí saw his tongue lying useless on the floor. He was humbled by a power greater than his own, and groveled before his father's feet. Olófin, seeing the same humility that Obí possessed while still human, felt sorry for the orisha. He said, "My son, once you were pure of heart, yet through time your ways toward others became evil. Somewhere, somehow, you lost the virtues of humility and charity for my children on earth. Yet I still find it in my heart to forgive you. For your crimes, your own aché has removed the power of speech, and with the mouth you will never utter another word; yet I shall give you back your speech in a different manner. If you ever want to communicate with another, you must first throw yourself to the floor as in foribale to me, and then shall your will be known to others.

"And since you have become all bright and beautiful on the outside, yet within have become dark and hard, a hypocrite, your appearance for an eternity shall be changed, and this is my punishment to you. A thick crust will mask your physical beauty like the one that exists within you now, yet hidden within will be the glow. This skin will be shed and the brightness seen only when you are called to serve another, for in service will you find your salvation. As you have become two-faced, good to the orisha and bad to the poor, so shall you have two faces. One will show your beauty in a glow, which was a gift from me that I can never entirely remove, and one will show your hypocrisy through darkness, an evil brought on yourself. From this day forth, no matter how dirty or vile those who question you, you are bound, Obí, always to speak the truth at their feet in humbleness. You will always be available to serve the other orishas, for they never failed to give alms to my children on earth, the poor and deformed."

Thus did his own hands and his father's give Obí's punishment, and Obí was bound to a life of servitude and truth forevermore.

Obí had once been human, a pure, modest man whose inner beauty so impressed Olófin that he was made an orisha, immortal. Inward beauty was brought without by Olódumare's blessings; he was stunning, radiant. Yet pride and vanity grew in those first centuries until, by his own actions, Obí fell from grace. No longer would he live in an opulent palace, nestled beyond the mortal realm. His new home was the coconut palm, a tree of modest height, well rooted in this earth. No longer was he dressed in scintillating white cloth. His form was dark and hard; he found himself thickly encrusted with a hairy shell. His beauty, a gift endowed to match his purity, was hidden by this shell, and masked again by a thick, rough skin born of his evil. Obí's musical voice was silenced through the ages: none would hear him speak, or sing, or even sigh. To communicate, the coconut was cursed to throw himself in foribale upon the earth and from this would letters open to make known his will.

After his fall from grace, Obí's new form came under Obatalá's ownership, for not only is he the guardian of things deformed, but he also is the owner of all whiteness. Because Olófin had decreed that Obí would work and speak on behalf of all the orishas as the world evolved, Obatalá was faced with the distribution of this gift to all of them. The spirits were called beneath one of Obí's trees, and there the king of the white cloth* laid out a nut broken into five pieces and said, "With this, the oracle of Obí, each of you will speak to our children on earth. Although the aché of this tree is mine, it is also mine to share with all of you. Know that Obí can never lie—either to you or for you—nor can he lie to those paying him homage by using the oracle. Obí will only speak the truth as he knows it." There, beneath the coconut tree, Obatalá taught the five secret signs by which Obí communicated between orishas and mortals. This was the beginning of his redemption, and the beginning of our oracle in Cuba.

In time, however, even the tree that bore Obí to earth was affected by vanity and pride, until Babaluaiye and Elegguá taught her again to be humble. This tale is titled "The Story of the Coconut Tree" and is told in Owani Ofún (11-10) of the *diloggún* (cowrie shell divination).

The Story of the Coconut Tree

A proud coconut palm once grew in the land of the orishas. Her leaves were thick, strong, and greener than the fronds of other trees. In the morning dew she was radiant; at night, by the moon's pale glow, she was luminescent. Other plants and trees looked at her with envy, for beauty was her aché. Time passed, and she filled with hundreds of coconuts. Their weight was a burden but their fruitfulness was a blessing. Arrogantly she stood contemplating herself, refusing to make *ebó* (an offering) in thankfulness for her

---

* "King of the white cloth" is a praise name for Obatalá. It is said that he created all things by spinning them from "white cloth."

wealth. "You must give some of your prosperity back to the earth," whispered the other trees, "lest she strike out and claim what is hers." Yet the coconut palm would hear none of this. "I am grand, the mother of all goodness in the forest," she said in self-deception. "My children, the coconuts, enjoy good health. Why make ebó when I am already blessed with beauty and fruitfulness? You all must make ebó to become more like me!" she taunted. Time passed, and as more of her children ripened, gentle pride turned to vanity.

It came to pass that when the coconut tree was most content with herself, the air moved violently. A strong wind gusted through the forest, and one of her many children fell to the earth. The trees stood still, amazed that such a thing happened, and for a moment even the coconut palm was frightened. Her self-delusion, however, had grown, and she called out to the forest, "Do not worry—it is not a bad omen. My friends, my child is ripe; he is a perfect seed born from my perfection. In time, my son will grow tall and handsome, and will stand proudly next to his mother. The blessings bestowed on the forest will be doubled." Lost again to herself and her coconuts, she gathered together her fronds to protect her fallen seed from the elements, to nurture him while he grew. While she was fawning over herself and her seed, the powerful orisha Babaluaiye came walking through the forest with Elegguá at his side. In kindness, the father of the earth saluted the tree, for her children, the coconuts, gave him the milk that he so loved. With his eyes closed, Babaluaiye payed foribale to her and the orisha that she bore; he did not notice that he was not saluted back. His kindness went unacknowledged.

"Father," whispered Eshu (Elegguá) in disbelief. "You are an orisha, yet you acknowledge a tree?"

"That tree is mother to our fallen Obí, and he, Elegguá, provides the coconut milk that I love. She is deserving of our respect, being the mother to one of our spirits."

"She deserves respect as you do, Father," Eshu said, interrupting. "Yet the tree did not salute you in return. She is ignoring your kind gestures and blessings. Did you not know that she has become proud and vain, so vile within that she does not make ebó to any of us in gratitude for her blessings? She is a selfish, self-absorbed creature, Father."

Babaluaiye saw the truth in Elegguá's words, and watched as the tree, lost in reverie, considered only herself. He had not been saluted; the palm had not even realized that she was saluted. Angry, Babaluaiye lifted his hand, pointed his finger at the tree, and said, "The worm within the coconut is known only to the coconut." Silently, he continued walking.

Elegguá remained behind in disbelief. He watched the tree for a moment. Unexpectedly, a single coconut fell to the ground. The palm was pleased until she realized, "He is not ripe!" Elegguá heard her frightened gasp and laughed; he then blew on the tree. Another unripe coconut fell, followed by another, until coconuts rained down upon the earth. The mighty tree shook in anger and fright, which only loosened more of her children from her grasp. Anger turned to horror as she watched the earth beneath her seem to boil; it was alive, writhing among her roots. Worms came crawling from the boiling earth, sensing a new source of food above their dens; and horror turned to pain as the worms not only ate her children, but also bore deep into her own bark. So quickly did they come that the proud, once beautiful tree was overwhelmed with sickness and fell down to the earth, dead. Because of the palm's vanity, all became victims of Babaluaiye's scourge, a terrible cancer that arose from the ground and overwhelmed the family of coconuts.

Elegguá was pleased.

It is through these three patakís that the story of Obí's evolution and eventual devolution is told: Purity granted him immortality; vanity caused his fall. Even his new mother, the coconut palm, was destined in time to fall because of pride. Alone, the immortal Obí has no aché, no apparent purpose in the scheme of creation. Perhaps this is why the centuries changed his nature from what he once was: selfless, pure, and noble. Yet after his fall he was given a purpose, a method of redemption and salvation. Once again he became the humble servant, the voice of the spirits on earth so that their followers could petition and question the forces that molded the world.

The Orisha Associated with Obí

Obí provides us with a link to the mighty ones; he gives us a channel through which to ask, to listen, and to carry out their will in the world. Ritually, we partake in his salvation whenever the oracle is opened. He may connect us with any orisha, but the ones with whom he most commonly works follow.

Elegguá

Elegguá is at once a young child and an old man; no matter his appearance, however, he is among the wisest of the orishas, knowing all things that lie in heaven and on earth. His worship and propitiation are essential to the practice of Santería, for without his goodwill there is nothing that can be done by any other spirit in the pantheon. Those who practice Obí divination normally direct most questions to this orisha before any other is approached, and even when directing divination at another spirit, Elegguá is still given his due worship and reverence. Where there are large gatherings of children, there Elegguá may be found; he is also present at all crossroads and roams the forest freely. He controls fate, decisions, and all aspects of life in which capriciousness or pure chance is a deciding factor. His sacred colors are red, black, and white; his numbers are said to be three, seven, and twenty-one (some houses include the number eleven). When invoked for Obí divination, most diviners will call him with a rattle.

Ogún

Ogún, blood brother to Elegguá, is another orisha whose worship is essential to the practice of Santería. He is known as the spirit of iron, the one who controls the vast stores of this mineral beneath the earth and who guides the hands of those who use it in their lives. He is a skilled blacksmith and craftsman, an excellent hunter, and a healer (the patron of doctors and surgeons, as their healing tools contain iron). There are few rituals that can be conducted in the religion without his aid. All sacrifices made to the orishas are directed first to Elegguá, yet it is only with Ogún's blessing that the sacrifice may be made at all. He is the knife that takes the life of the animal, or the hand that guides it, and when Elegguá or any other orisha is to eat, Ogún must be given his first taste. Although this orisha is said to roam the wilds and the forest, he is also found in areas where there are large stores of iron ore or where large amounts of iron are used (such as railroad tracks). He also is present in every city, for it is he who created the basis for all civilization. Many also credit this spirit with humanity's evolution from the hunting/gathering phase to the husbandry/agricultural age, as Ogún is the one who creates all farming tools and implements. The shift from an agrarian society to one of industrialization was also directed by Ogún's hands, as iron formed the basis for that as well. Ogún's sacred colors are said to be green, black, and white; his numbers are three, seven, and twenty-one. Most will use a rattle to call him during Obí divination.

Ochosi

Ochosi is the master of all *ewe* (herbs), of the forest, and of all animals that live within. Beyond Ogún, there is no orisha who can rival his skills at the hunt. Being adept at witchcraft (using herbs), many of this faith who practice their skills at *brujería* (Spanish for "witchcraft") depend on Ochosi to empower their work. Although this powerful spirit resides in the forest, his true mansion is the jail, the place where felons are incarcerated for their crimes against humanity. Ochosi is justice; his arrows plunge deeply into the hearts of criminals, and when offended by mortals' actions, he punishes them by incarcerating them. Many of his *eboses* (offerings) are left at the doors to the jail. When he is not there, this orisha prefers to spend all his time in the forest, practicing his skills at the hunt with his crossbow and arrow, a gift created for him by Obatalá, whom Ochosi adores. This orisha's sacred colors are said to be blue and gold; his numbers are twenty-one, seven, and three. When invoked for Obí divination, most will call him with the rattle.

In the Lucumí pantheon, these three orishas are perhaps the most important. It is said that Elegguá, Ogún, and Ochosi form the foundation of the faith. So strong is their link and so important is their aché to the worshiper that the reception of these three spirits is mandated for *aleyos* (noninitiates) in an initiation known as the reception of the warriors. During this lengthy ritual, the orishas Elegguá, Ogún, and Ochosi are prepared in a ceremony known as the *lavatorio*. Using special herbs, an elixir called *omiero* is created. The three spirits and their tools are washed in this, and by secret rituals are given life by an aleyo's godparents. With them is washed another orisha, named Ósun. This spirit has no voice of his own and does not speak through Obí or any other religious oracle; his sole purpose is to watch over the recipient night and day, falling to his side or ringing his bells when danger is near. The birthing ceremonies are lengthy, but the actual reception is short. The aleyo is presented to his orishas, and three days after their birth is allowed to take them home. Twenty-one days after their initial washing, the warriors are given a ritual of entrada (entrance) into the devotee's home. This consists of a meal for the orishas: Two roosters and two pigeons are fed to them. One week after this, a basket of cool fruits is given. Once all these things have been done, the warriors are seated in the client's life, and he can begin his lifelong relationship with them. *Note:* Once an aleyo has received the warriors, technically he is no longer an aleyo; he is an *aborisha*, one who worships the orishas, although he is not yet crowned a priest.

Elegguá, being destiny, fate, and the messenger of all spirits, is the most important of the three. His worship and propitiation are essential if the aborisha hopes to evolve in the religion and in life. Ogún stands behind Elegguá, a powerful warrior who is ready to strike down the enemies of the devoted; wielding his machete, Ogún fights tirelessly, ceaselessly to cut down the things that stand in the way of one's evolution. Yet Ogún is random and wanton; it takes the wisdom of Ochosi, the hunter and tracker, to show Ogún where his force will serve the most good. Under Ochosi's direction, Ogún's force is used for the higher good, never for evil. With these three spirits working for the aborisha, there is almost nothing in life that cannot be obtained through hard work and perseverance. Many times, under the watchful eyes of his or her godparents, an aleyo will need to use Obí to divine with his spirits. Although this is a right that all who have received orishas have, it is not used lightly, and is always done under the guidance of elders. The reception of the warriors, however, does give one the right to divine with those spirits using Obí.

The next three orishas I will discuss (Ibeyi, Olokun, and Babaluaiye) are also spirits that may be received outside the initiation known as *asiento*. Just as the warriors of Ogún, Ochosi, Elegguá, and Ósun form the foundation for the faith, these three orishas add to the aché of the aborisha, and are often given to offer stability, strength, and evolution in life. Each fulfills a specific function in Olódumare's designs; they each have their own aché, and each may be questioned using Obi.

The Ibeyi

The Ibeyi are a sum of seven sacred Spirits, the children of miraculous birth, as orisha adherents know them. The term itself, however, is normally applied to the first two Spirits born, the twins Taewó and Kaindé. In the patakís, one learns that they are the illegitimate children of Shangó born from Oshún's womb; however, they were raised by Yemayá and blessed with great gifts by the mighty Obatalá. At one time, the birth of twins was considered a serious offense in Yoruba culture, but when the fourth king of Oyó, Shangó, had twins by one of his concubine wives, they gained prominence as harbingers of blessings and the cult of the Ibeyi came to prominence. With all the powers of Obatalá, Yemayá,

Oshún, and Shangó combined, their aché is so strong they are capable of miracles where only desperation may be found. Their sacred colors are those of their parents: white, blue, yellow, and red. They prefer dishes made in doubles, or twins, and all offerings given to them must be doubled and exactly alike. They are the patrons of children, of twins, and of the mothers of twins. When invoked for Obí divination, they are called with twin rattles. In Santería, it is not uncommon for these two orishas to be received by aborishas. Once received, even an aborisha without *ocha* (spirits) on his head has the right to divine with them using Obí.

Olokun

Olokun is an orisha who is feared, yet revered. She (some say he, for Olokun is androgynous) lives in the depths of the ocean, chained there from land by the mighty Obatalá. Before the earth was divided into land and sea, there was only water, a vast abyss that covered all things. Olokun ruled everything that lay beneath her waters. Olódumare sent Obatalá down from heaven onto a single peak of land, Orisha Oke,* the one point that Olokun could not cover. On this tiny pinnacle Obatalá had room to set one hen, and this hen scratched so furiously that earth was sent out over the void. In a rage, Olokun set out to destroy the land the hen created, but Obatalá offered her a gift from God: a large golden chain. Momentarily appeased, Olokun put this on; it wrapped about her tightly, weighing her down and sending her straight to the depths of her own kingdom. Gravity was born, land was born, and the waters were forced to recede upon themselves. Too vast to be restrained but unable to resist the supreme deity's sanctions, Olokun still ruled vast portions of the earth.

Water reigns supreme, even today, and land occupies only a small portion of the planet's surface. From her chaining, the parts of her aché that were too strong to be contained broke away, and

---

*Orisha Oke is the spirit of this mountain and gives his name to this mountain itself.

Yemayá arose from the waves, the owner of all fresh water that rains down upon the earth. This orisha may be received by aborishas who have not yet been initiated as priests or priestesses; worship and propitiation of this powerful spirit bring foundation and stability to one's life. Her color is the same as that of Yemayá, blue. Her metal is lead, for that is the only metal that cannot be corroded by the ocean. When called for Obí divination (she is consulted only on the most dire of needs), she is invoked with the circular shaking of a maraca.

Babaluaiye

Also known as Asohano, this orisha is one of the most feared and loved in the Lucumí pantheon. Those who adore him know this spirit as the father of infectious disease, the owner of smallpox and all afflictions of the skin. The arrival of HIV is attributed to this orisha as well. Although feared in Africa, he is beloved in Cuba and the United States, for just as he can afflict, so can he heal. As a force in nature, Asohano brings disease and death, the natural processes that destroy the weak and elderly so new life can flourish. Disease is not inevitable or incurable, however; this orisha also brings sanitation and hygiene and empowers modern medicine. The use of vaccinations to overcome disease is one of this spirit's miracles. A weakened form of a disease is inoculated into the body, and because it is something that cannot kill, it only makes the recipient stronger. By his work, the entire race is strengthened as it evolves.

Unlike the other orishas whose rituals may be done during the day, Babaluaiye's worship takes place only at night, in near darkness. He abhors water and substitutes coconut milk for it. Among his sacred attributes are the colors brown, black, purple, and yellow and the number seventeen. He is invoked with the cowbell during Obí divination. Just as the Ibeyi and Olokun are sometimes given to aleyos in this faith, so can Babaluaiye be received by those who are not priests and priestesses. His aché helps us attain and keep good health. Those who have this orisha are sometimes called

Lazareros (a name derived from San Lazaro, the Catholic persona for Asohano), and these have the right to divine with the orisha using Obí.

The next orishas may be taken only by those who have ocha done. The first five—Obatalá, Yemayá, Oshún, Oyá, and Shangó—are given in the ritual known as asiento. This is the initiation that confers aché upon an aborisha, transforming that person from a noninitiate to a iyawó, a bride of the spirits. The orisha who rules this person is crowned on the head, and the iyawó is then said to be a priest or priestess of that spirit. The asiento itself is lengthy and complicated, a series of rituals that begins with the shaving of one's head and the coronation or crowning of the initiate and ends seven days later when the iyawó emerges from the initiation room to begin his lifelong relationship with the orishas. For a year this iyawó loses his name among his peers and is referred to by his title exclusively, Iyawó. During this time he lives under the strictest taboos: Clothing, food, recreation, and travel are all limited and monitored severely. He or she is regarded as a child, a mere baby in the religion, and is treated accordingly until the year of taboo is complete. Although the iyawó does have the orishas in his home, he cannot divine with them; he cannot work with them at all except under the strict supervision of his godparents. It is during this time that most of the prayers, customs, and rituals of the religion are learned.

Obatalá

Beyond Olófin, Olorún, and Olódumare, there is no orisha greater than Obatalá. His name translates into "the King of the White Cloth." It was he (some know him as she) who first came to earth and stood upon the only visible peak, Orisha Oké (the mountain), chaining Olokun to the depths and creating land. It was he who fashioned humans from clay. It was he who, with Yembo/Yemayá, gave birth to all the orishas that could not descend on their own from heaven to earth. Owner of consciousness and human heads, and all are born to be his children, yet only his chosen can be initiated into his mysteries. Infants born with deformities are said to be Obatalá's by right of birth, as are those that come in the uterine sack. As he is responsible for the human condition, those who become impaired, injured, or elderly are under his special care. For his sacred colors, Obatalá claims white (although he shares it freely with the other orishas) along with red, purple, and green. Eight and sixteen are his numbers, and some attribute four to him as well. For his musical instrument, he is called with the *agogó,* a silver bell topped with a silver pigeon feather. He is consulted with Obí only on matters of great importance unless the supplicant is his child; he then responds amiably to all questions.

Yemayá

Those who know her know Yemayá as the owner of all fresh water upon the earth. She was born from the chaining of Olokun. The vastness of the oceans could not be held in one place, yet the golden chains of Olódumare could not be broken. Part of that orisha split away, and Yemayá arose from the foaming waves as one of the firstborn orishas. She is mother to all, and never denies the heart-felt pleas of those who come to her for comfort or support. She is not a doting mother, however. She is vengeful and wrathful when moved to anger. Yemayá may be found in the seas, the lakes, and the rain. It is she who fills the home of her sister, Oshún's rivers, with fresh, life-giving water. Her color is blue and among her attributes are the number seven, the metals silver and lead, and sweet molasses. When called for Obí divination, she is invoked with a circular shaking of a maraca.

Oshún

After all things were created in heaven and on earth, Olódumare looked down on what he had done. Worried that there could be more, or that there should be more to life than what he offered the first mortals, he created Oshún to embody all the sweetness, beauty, and love that he might have left out. It soon came to pass that there was none more awesome than she. This orisha incorporates love, beauty, eroticism, fertility, abundance, sweetness, and all those things that make life worth living. She is a mistress of dance, of magic, and of laughter, and bestows her blessings freely to those who worship her. Among her many attributes are the numbers five and twenty-five, and the color yellow belongs to her exclusively. Her metals are gold and brass. Honey, perfume, and mirrors are all given to her as devotions. When called down for divination with Obí, a brass bell is used as her musical instrument.

Oyá

Oyá is a woman of many talents. She is a warrior (and in this guise many know her as the bearded lady). She is the ruler of the marketplace, a symbol that means not only the market from which goods are purchased but also the world in which we live. She is the lady of the tornado (shared with her sister Ayaó, who is the tornado) and the harbinger of death. She keeps the gate of the cemetery opened or closed at will (the dead go through her gates into the hands of Oba, and then to Yewá, who is the grave. And there, the body is fed upon first by her, and then by Orisha Oko). She is concubine to Shangó, yet lover to none. Oyá rules whirlwinds, storms, and the lightning that flashes across the darkened sky. Among her sacred attributes are all colors (brought together for a total of nine), the number nine, copper, and the seedpod of the flame tree, which is used to call her for Obí divination. Boomerangs, pinwheels, and masks are also hers, and many of these may be found at her shrines.

Shangó

Shangó is an interesting spirit among the orishas. It is said that in either the eleventh or twelfth century, he was a mortal who ruled as the fourth king of the city-state Oyó. While bringing peace and unity to the Yoruba nation, Shangó himself became corrupt, pitting his two brothers against each other until one was killed. In shame, the man took himself to the forest to end his own life. The manner of execution among the Yoruba was primarily hanging, and Shangó planned to take his own life this way. However, the force of his prior good deeds and his own efforts to right his wrongs inspired pity from the orishas, and it is said that the king did not hang—he ascended to become orisha. Other legends hold that this orisha was born from Yemayá when she brought the immortals to earth through her own womb. Most agree that Shangó is Irunmole himself, one of the firstborn orishas, yet incarnated among mortals to experience life. His sacred colors are red and white; his numbers are four, six, and twelve. When invoked for Obí divination, most priests and priestesses will use the rattle as his sacred instrument.

Yewá

Of all the orishas, this is the only one who never married, never loved (physically), and never gave birth to another spirit on earth. This child of Obatalá was stunning; such were her charms that Shangó fell in love with her, even though he knew Obatalá hoped she would stay virgin and chaste forever. Out of love, he gave her a beautiful fire opal, and her father Obatalá found her with this. Knowing that such a gift could come only from Shangó, he forever parted the two orishas. Yewá was sent to live in the cemetery among the spirits of the dead, cursed to remain there for eternity. Shangó, who is afraid of the dead, would never again see her. It is rare that a priestess receives this orisha, for her reception all but guarantees that a woman will never love again. So bitter is Yewá over her losses that she keeps chaste and pure those she loves and guards. Women wait until long after they are in secure marriages, and long after menopause, before receiving her mysteries. Men almost never have her, for she regards all men with suspicion. Although she may go to the head of an initiate (she does have her own small priesthood), she is made only to women, and only a daughter of Oshún or Yewá herself can perform these rituals. Many give her Obí at a graveyard (beside a grave's bed) when making ebó to her, determining if the offering has been accepted. Unless one actually has this orisha living in the home, it is taboo to approach her for any other reason.

Oba

Once Shangó and Yewá were parted, Obatalá decreed Oba the legitimate wife of Shangó. They married, then lived together for many years. During this time Shangó became enamored with both Oshún and Oyá, and carried on affairs with these two orishas. Oshún, jealous of Oba, once told her that if she wanted to keep her husband, she had to cut off her own ear and serve it to him in a soup so that he would be bound to her forever. Oba did this, and so angry was her husband that he cursed her to live among the dead. There, Oba grew spiritually and physically, and became one of the strongest female orishas in the pantheon. After many centuries passed, she arose refreshed and became the woman who punishes those who harm women. She became the patroness of the home, of education, of learning, and of writing. When women are desperate for help, when writers are desperate for inspiration, when someone seeks forbidden or arcane knowledge, these people turn to Oba, who learned all wisdom from the dead. She has her own small priesthood, and although many argue the point in the religion, only women can be made as her priestesses; she will not go to the head of a man without severely changing his masculine energies (some priests made to her become transgendered and transsexuals).

Orisha Oko

Orisha Oko is a dark, mysterious spirit; he does have a priesthood, but it is small. The secrets for crowning him on the head are lost to most lines of the faith beyond Cuba. He is alive and well in the religion, however, and is normally received as an *adimú* orisha, one who is not crowned but is received by priests and priestesses after the initiation of asiento. Spiritually, it is said that Oko is a child of the earth itself, born when the oceans receded. He is the husband of Olokun in some patakís; others pair him with Olosa (the lagoon) or Yemayá. Said to be incredibly handsome during the day, his form is equally horrible during the night; he embodies the fecundity and decay of the earth, and his mysteries encapsulate all her cycles. Physically, Oko is said to have incarnated among mortals in the ancient city of Irawo. He was the king, and ruled over his subjects before the discoveries of agriculture. During his reign on earth, Oko became afflicted with leprosy and was banished by his subjects. The monarch's wife was loyal to him and left with her husband to wander the countryside.

In time, through dreams, Oko discovered the secrets of planting, raising, and harvesting crops, and as he mastered these skills, his leprosy was healed. Returning to Irawo with his new secrets, he was reinstated as ruler. In return, he taught his subjects the secrets of agriculture, and the city became firmly established and wealthy under his rule. After his death many decades later, Oko became known as Orisha Oko, the patron of farmers, throughout Irawo and the rest of the Yoruba nation. This spirit has become associated with the colors pink and blue, and is received in the form of a farmer plowing with an ox. The *otá* (sacred stone) for him is white, and is found in a freshly plowed field. His stone is exposed, not sealed in a *sopera* (bowl), but his diloggún is kept inside a tiny tureen beside his shrine. No numbers are directly associated with him. He is called with a delicately beaded maraca for Obí divination.

TWO

The Principles of Casting Obí

OBÍ'S LIFE, like the lives of all the other orishas, is recorded in the diloggún, an oral, sacred literature comprising 256 *odu* (patterns). His story begins in Obara Osá (6–9). It is here that one learns of a mortal Obí, elevated and granted immortality by Olófin. Although selfless and pure as a mortal, centuries of eternal life changed the orisha. His ego and vanity grew until his heart was hard. Harsh words spoken to the father of creation caused him to lose his tongue; it fell from his mouth as he groveled for forgiveness. The hardness of Obí's heart encased him like a shell. His outward beauty was bound within, and Olófin cursed him to an eternity of servitude. The shining Obí was transformed into the coconut and a new divination system was born. To regain his speech, Obí was forced to speak in five mysterious signs; to find his salvation, he was bound to serve all on earth. Obatalá was given the task of distributing the oracle among all the spirits in heaven. Beneath a coconut palm, he showed the orishas the five basic patterns by which the fallen spirit could communicate their desires to mortals. One task still remained: the dissemination of this knowledge to the human race. That task also fell to Obatalá; and the story of the first coconut diviners is told in the odu Oché Metanla (5–13) in the diloggún.

Biague: the Birth of Divination with the Coconut

Obí had fallen, the once shining immortal now swathed in a dark, unyielding shell. Cursed for his arrogance and sins against Olófin and humanity, he was forced to serve or forever remain silent. By Olófin's wisdom was a system devised, a series of five basic patterns that could be used by those who knew the oracle's secrets. First, Obatalá taught the orishas the letters of Obí. Once they had that knowledge, he was faced with a greater challenge: to teach humans how to divine with the oracle, a task he knew not how to complete. The earth was teeming with life, and the ranks of those who adored the orishas grew daily. There were many who could benefit from the knowledge, but Obatalá was just one orisha, and there were just too many for him to teach.

While the spirit pondered these things, in a town called Ilé Ilú, a young man named Biague was crowned a priest of Obatalá. He was a simple man who delighted in modest pleasures, and his asiento was the most profound moment of his life. Those at *itá* told the iyawó that the mysteries of odu were not his; he would never have the aché to divine with the shells. Barred from divination, the iyawó lamented that his initiation would never benefit anyone but himself. He would have no way to divine, to placate or mark ebó to the orishas; he could help none achieve his destiny. Nightly this priest would pray to his spirits, "If only I could divine. If only I could help others. Nothing else matters." Obatalá was touched by the iyawó's cries, and when the year of cleansing was over, the orisha came to Biague and taught him the secrets of Obí. Patiently were the five signs revealed, and then the more subtle patterns within those signs. Obatalá taught Biague how to pray, how to praise, and how to placate. This was a new oracle, and because no other mortal on earth had its secrets, the young priest soon found fame and fortune with his skills.

Having wealth, Biague decided to marry and raise a family. He chose his wife and soon the two had a son they named Adiatoto. Once he was weaned, the couple sought to have another child, but Biague's wife died in labor and the baby with her. The priest's love for her was so deep that he never remarried, yet his desire for a large family was so strong that he began to adopt orphans. Each of these loved the diviner dearly, for he had saved them from lives of poverty and despair. Time on the streets had made their hearts hard, however, and while fond of Biague, they loathed Adiatoto, his natural son. When no one was around to hear them, they were cruel to the young child and taunted him, saying, "You are almost as us, without a mother. We are all the same!" To these things the old diviner was blind; his heart never healed from the death of his wife, and his work kept him busy.

In time, Obí told Biague that his life was coming to an end. Not wanting the oracle's secrets to die with him, Biague chose to give his only true son, Adiatoto, the knowledge of his oracle. This was his most prized possession, and the one secret that had made him rich.

For many weeks Biague sat patiently with his boy, remembering as he did the time when Obí and Obatalá had first taught him the secret patterns of the oracle. Slowly, laboriously, the father revealed these patterns in turn, showing Adiatoto how the humbled spirit Obí would always talk and speak in truth at the feet of all who questioned him. This conversation between human and orisha relies on five special patterns, and within these letters are more subtle patterns that the boy struggled to master before he could learn to cast the oracle on his own. There were prayers to learn, patakís to master, and praise names to call. This and more Biague's son learned, for he was gifted with brilliance. As the lessons drew to a close, Biague realized that Obí had taken well to his child. The boy had acquired the aché to divine all things in heaven and on earth.

"You are blessed by Olófin and all the orishas; Obí has found favor with you," said the father with pride. "Keep the gift dear to your heart, and always respect the orisha Obí. It is a gift that I give to you and only you, my son." Not long after this, Biague died of sudden illness, and Adiatoto's adopted brothers, jealous of the divine gift their father had given the boy, stole all his earthly goods because he was in possession of the divine. "We bar you from this house," they said. "The old man loved you more, and all your life you were spoiled. Now you are as we, without mother and father. Go out and learn to take care of yourself, as we did for so many years. If you ever come back or try to steal what is ours, we will kill you!" The adopted brothers then continued to live on their father's land while Adiatoto was forced to wander. Frightened, he left his hometown of Ilé Ilú altogether, and soon took up a nomadic existence in a neighboring village.

Adiatoto spent many years in poverty, scraping together a living with his skills at divination. Obí provided the basic necessities of life and the young man was grateful for that. Using the oracle innumerable times, he grew strong in its practice, and the amount of information he was able to glean with just four pieces of raw coconut left his clients astounded. As he wandered it came to pass that the village king wanted to buy new land in Ilé Ilú for a larger, more opulent palace and he coveted the acres once owned by Adiatoto's father. The king sent forth his guards to find the owners of the land, and the greedy brothers, who still lived on the estate, came forward to sell the property.

On their quest the guards had discovered that the land was once owned by the famous diviner Biague, and that although the adopted sons lived there, no one knew for sure if they owned it. There were rumors of a missing boy, Biague's true son, Adiatoto, who had disappeared into the country upon his father's death. Some said he had met with treachery, others believed he left because of a broken heart. Hearing these things, the king demanded proof of the brothers' claim to the diviner's estate, but they admitted that they had none. From a neighboring village, Adiatoto had heard about the king's desires from one of his own clients, and decided to go to the palace to plead his case for his father's land.

The guards, recognizing the name, escorted him before the king. The monarch was still demanding proof of ownership from Adiatoto's adopted brothers.

Humbly, the young diviner came before him: "Your majesty," he said, "I have no proof, but I am the legal heir of my father; my adopted brothers stole everything from me and left me in poverty to wander the countryside. Although I have no legal papers, there is a way that we can determine the true owner of Biague's estate."

"And what might that be?" the king asked. The brothers became nervous, muttering among themselves as Adiatoto explained his father's profession and the secrets he had left him. "No one but my father knew how to divine with this oracle," said the young man, "and of all who worship and adore the orishas, he taught its secrets only to me." The proof Adiatoto offered was in the testing of the oracle. He would allow the king to ask any one question of Obí, a question to which only he would know the answer. If the oracle passed this test, they would then use it to determine the true owner of Biague's belongings. If the oracle failed and proved fraudulent, Adiatoto would give up his claim to the land and the king could negotiate with his brothers.

In testing the oracle, the king asked not just one but several questions; and each time the oracle answered not only yes or no but in the seasoned hands of Adiatoto also revealed many secrets the king did not know. After a lengthy line of questioning, the mighty monarch was satisfied of its truth. "It speaks well. Let it decide who is the true owner of Biague's land so that I may buy it," he said. One by one, Adiatoto threw the oracle at the feet of his adopted brothers, and Obí ruled out each of them. Then Adiatoto threw it for himself, and Obí answered that he was the true owner. Thus did the brothers lose their rights to the entire estate for their treachery, and Adiatoto negotiated a sale that made him a very wealthy man. Impressed by his skills as a diviner, the king employed Adiatoto as his personal consultant. Prosperity and abundance were his all the days of his life, as the entire town sought him out for help in all their problems.

Preparing to Use Obí

Having learned the patakís in odu that support this divination system, we now follow the path of Adiatoto as he learned this oracle from his father, Biague. The mechanics, prayers, and praise names must be committed to memory before the first throw of the coconut, for to toss an orisha to the floor haphazardly is disrespectful, and although minor, Obí is still an orisha.

As with any other religious practice, there are special rules to follow when one prepares this oracle for use. Realize that although an aleyo who has received an orisha may question that spirit with the coconuts, the godparents should first be approached with the question. Depending on the nature of the consultation, and also on the orisha being consulted, different patterns will carry different shades of meaning, and these subtleties should be considered. If the diviner is inexperienced with the oracle and is questioning a mysterious orisha such as Olokun, Orisha Oko, or Naná Burukú, a godparent may wish to be present during the consultation to offer advice.

Second, one must be pure and clean before approaching the orishas. Never open an oracle after sexual relations; this is an offense to these spirits, for they embody pure forces. Sexual energies, while earthly reflections of spiritual mechanics, quickly degenerate after copulation is complete. Menstruating women should not open Obí, for blood is life, spiritually hot, and divination requires coolness lest the forces one seeks to pacify are provoked. The coconut itself is a cool seed, and seeks to maintain that coolness. It will be overwhelmed by those in these spiritual states. Anyone whose essence is volatile should bathe thoroughly from head to toe, and then the oracle may be opened.

Once these important prohibitions have been observed, take a coconut and shake it to see that it is fresh. If the fruit is ripe, you will hear milk sloshing within. Having found a fresh one, hold the nut in the left hand and a strong, blunt striking instrument (such as a hammer) in the right. Obí, being both an orisha and a voice for the orishas, must now be given proper respect. Ask his permission to open the shell. Do not place him on the floor, nor should you strike him on a hard surface—these are major offenses to the coconut spirit. Say the words "Agó, Obí" before you strike, then try to crack the shell in one swift blow. *Agó* is the Lucumí word for "with your permission." By asking this first, we show reverence to the coconut.

The milk will flow freely, and some try to collect as much of it as possible to bathe the *orí* (head), bringing coolness and freshness to it. The milk must be used quickly or not at all, for it soon becomes sour and loses its aché. Setting the juices aside for later use, examine the interior of the coconut. Freshness is evident in the firm, smooth, wet whiteness of the meat. Pry out the largest pieces possible, keeping intact the black skin that rests against the shell. Cut these pieces into five large, rounded parts. Four of these will be used in the actual process of divination; set aside the fifth in case one breaks. Keep in mind that on rare occasions Obí can become heated. When this happens, all five pieces will have to be oiled and taken to the street to banish the bad letters from the house. Because his tongue was destroyed by his harsh words to Olófin, the orisha Obí is limited in speech. If, during a session, the diviner has not the aché to determine what the spirit is saying, his frustration turns into negative signs that will need to be removed from the house. A few extra coconuts should always be kept in reserve for this purpose. The orisha must be cooled, silenced for a time, and the oracle renewed in freshness. Having cut the oracle, place the five parts in a round white plate. A white bowl of cool, fresh water should be set in the center of this. The oracle is now prepared for use.

There is an important point that must be kept in mind about the oracle: Obí is not a spiritual tool to be used at the diviner's whim. Obí is an orisha, a god, and must be treated with the utmost respect during the divination process. Because one has opened this god to question and petition even more powerful gods, frivolity is to be avoided. As a diviner, you should have the central point of this session, the question to which an answer is desired, framed firmly in your mind. Next, examine the question that is going to be asked. What is the hoped-for response? The question must be asked in such a way that the most positive response can be given, "Yes, the world is in balance," for the strongest letter of this oracle, Ejife, means just that: The world is in balance. If the question cannot be answered in this manner, it must be rephrased. For example, if I were considering to move out of state for a new job, the question "Will I be making a mistake if I move for this job?" would not be properly phrased. In this case, if the oracle answers with a basic "Yes, all is well," there will be confusion. Is Obí saying, "Yes, it is a mistake," or is Obí saying, "Yes, the world is in balance." Likewise, a basic no would be just as confusing, for it could mean "Do not move" or "No, it would not be good to stay." The question should be phrased, "I want to move for a new job that has been offered [here, the purpose of the divination has been clearly stated]; will all be well with this?" Now the question has been asked so that the most positive response will be yes. Or, more simply, I could ask, "Should I make the move for the new job that has been offered?" Phrasing the question so the most positive answer is yes avoids confusion from Obí.

The final point for the novice to consider is this: The orishas have personalities and free will. Like humans, they do display displeasure and express anger, although never when undeserved. If you are about to divine and believe the orisha petitioned has issues pending, do not divine at that time. The orisha might use the oracle to bring punishment and, hence, balance. For example: If I once promised Elegguá a basket of fruit if he brought a specific blessing and did not deliver the fruit when the blessing was received, he would be displeased. Anything gleaned from the divination might be his way of exacting punishment, removing the blessing, or getting the votive offering he deserved. Some who divine will infrequently place a special offering with the orisha a few hours before the divination session to cool, placate, and sweeten the spirits. The answers of Obí are more than answers—they are openings for spiritual forces to enter our lives, and these doors, once opened, cannot be closed. That is why a skilled diviner will never ask an improperly phrased question or ask the same question twice: To do so is to confuse and mock the powers with which we work.

Having prepared the oracle and observed these rules, stand before the orisha to be questioned. Pick up four rounded coconut pieces with the left hand and with the right hand sprinkle three dashes of water on the floor. While giving this libation to cool and refresh the orishas, say:

Omi tutu; ona tutu, aché tutu. Tutu ilé.
Tutu Laroye. Tutu arikú babawa.

Fresh water; freshen the road, freshen my power. Freshen my home. Freshen Elegguá [Eshu Laroye]. Freshness that has no end, freshness so that we do not see an early death.

Before we pray to any orisha, this simple libation is offered to bring coolness and freshness: to our roads, to our aché, to our homes, and to Eshu Laroye. The world is a place of hot and cold, stagnation and refreshment, growth and decline. When working with the orishas, however, we put ourselves in a place where only evolution can be found. Those things that tend to overheat and destroy are removed. A very special path of Elegguá, Eshu Laroye, is both honored and refreshed by this ritual gesture. He is the companion of Oshún, the orisha who makes life worth living, and is one of Elegguá's most mischievous paths. If we desire our prayers to reach the orishas, we must first honor and cool him so that he will help, and not hinder, our communication. It takes only a moment to do this, yet it is one of the most crucial points in our invocation. Having refreshed ourselves, our homes, and Eshu Laroye, the ritual of *mojubando* begins. As the *mojuba* (prayer) is chanted, use the thumbnail of the right hand to break off small slivers of the coconuts being held in the left hand. These slivers are saved and used later as a cool offering to the orisha being questioned. Although some houses dictate that the number of slivers removed be equal to the sacred numbers of the orisha questioned, this is not a necessity. All that is required is to remove at least three slivers from each rounded slice of coconut, for three is the number of Elegguá, who opens the roads to the divine. While the mojuba is chanted, another person may sound the orisha's sacred instrument to help in the process of invocation.

Mojuba Olófin. Mojuba Olorún. Mojuba Olódumare. Mojuba Olójoni. Oní odún mocuedun. Olorún alabosúdaye. Olorún alabosúnife. Olorún alayé. Olorún elemí. Olódumare oba aterere kaje. Olódumare, mojuba gbogbo ikú imbelese. Olódumare, ibaé bayé tonú. Mojuba atijó ojo. Mojuba atiwó orún. Mojuba ayái odún, oní odún, odún olá. Mojuba orún. Mojuba oshúkua. Mojuba ile ogere a foko jerí.

Homage is paid to the part of God closest to the earth. I pay homage to the God in the heavens, God who is eternal and everywhere. I pay homage to the one who owns this day. Today I greet you! Olorún, who is the keeper and protector of the earth. Olorún, the one who protects the first, holy city of Ifé. Olorún, living one and owner of the earth. Olorún, you who owns all spirits. Olódumare, the one who encompasses the entire cosmos. Olódumare, I give homage to all the ancestors that sit at your feet now. I praise the creative forces and those that have sacrificed their own lives for the continuity of life. I pay homage to the awakening sun, the sunrise. I pay homage to the dying sun, the sunset. I pay homage to all eternity: yesterday, today, and tomorrow. I pay homage to the sun. I pay homage to the moon. I pay homage to Mother Earth.

To invoke a specific spiritual force, first render praise to the greater power from which all is descended. The mojuba begins by addressing these three entities: Olófin, Olorún, and Olódumare. Olófin is a Lucumí contraction meaning "owner of the palace." It is the name given to the oldest Obatalá, whom some consider to be God on earth. Earth is the palace to which the phrase refers; it is the dwelling of the deities, the omnipresent forces that created all things, and also the home of the orishas who are born from God and the earth. Olorún is the second power given praise. This is also a contraction, denoting "the owner of heaven." Olorún is seen in the daytime sky. He is the sun, and although one does not worship the sun, praise is given to it as the symbol of God on earth. Finally praise is given Olódumare, whose name means "owner of the womb" or "owner of odu." Although Olódumare is referred to as androgynous, many have come to know this force as a mothering principle. Its essence is nurturing and its action is to give birth. Having honored those forces that began creation, the mojuba continues to acknowledge the first sacred things to descend from this womb and the beginning of wisdom and the Yoruba empire. The prayer now continues to acknowledge the influence of those who perpetuated the spiritual traditions of our faith, the religious elders who lived and died in service to Olódumare and the orishas.

> **Mojuba gbogbowan olodo araorún: Oluwo, Iyalocha, Babalosha, omo-kolaba egun imbelese Olódumare.**
> **Mojuba gbogbowan olodo araorún: Oluwo, Iyalocha, Babalosha, omo-kolaba egun Elelegba* lagba lagba imbelese, timbelese Olódumare.**

> *I pay homage to those who have gone to the river and who are now citizens of heaven, the dead priests and priestesses who rest with Olódumare. I pay homage to all the Oluwos, Iyalochas,*

---

* This is a Lucumí contraction meaning "the dead priest/esses of Elegguá." For the other orishas, put "Ol" or "Olo" directly before a name and say it as one word. Examples: Olobatala, Oloshun, Oloya, Ologun, Olochosi. In the case of orishas who are not crowned on the head, but are given *oro* in Santo, a hyphenated word in used. *Omo,* which means "child," is hyphenated onto the name of the orisha. Examples: Omo-Ibeyi, Omo-Aina, Omo-Babaluaiye, Omo-Inle. For the dead of Yemayá and Shangó, the proper contraction to use is "Oniyemayá" and "Onishangó."

Babaloshas, and Babalawos who have Olófin, the dead who are at the feet of God. I pay homage to those who have gone to the river who are now citizens of heaven: Oluwo, Iyalocha, Babalosha, Babalawos who have Olófin, and also to the dead of Eleggúa who are now at the feet of God.

Having given homage to the powers of creation, the dead elders, and the dead priests and priestesses of the orisha being questioned, it is now important to mojuba to the ancestors of the religious and blood family. We say that we stand on the shoulders of those who have come before; and even though it is an orisha whom we question, we would not be consulting with this orisha had not our ancestors given birth to us physically or spiritually. The next part of the chant calls on their strength, their knowledge, and their aché before invoking the macrocosmic forces we know as orisha.

Ibaé bayen tonú gbogbo egun ará orún orí emi nani [your name in ocha or your given name if ocha has not been made].

I give homage to all the ancestral forces that join me on my journey, I who am known as _____.

Ibaé bayen tonú gbogbo egun ará orún orí iyá [or babá] tobi mi [name of your godparent].

Ibaé bayen tonú gbogbo egun ará orún orí yubonna mi [name of your yubonna].

Ibaé bayen tonú gbogbo egun ará orún orí igboro kale ile.

I pay my homage and give my respect to all the ancestors that accompany the priests and priestesses visiting my house.

Ibaé bayen tonú gbogbo egun, gbogbowan olodó, lagba lagba otokú Ará orún timbelaye, imbelese Olorún, Olódumare.

I give my respect and pay homage to all the dead, to all those who have gone to the river and are now my spiritual ancestors; I pay homage to all those in heaven who bow at the feet of Olódumare.

Araorún, ibaé bayen tonú [name of deceased priest or priestess] ibaé.

Those who now live in heaven, my respects are paid to those who have gone to the other land in the sky [name of deceased priest/ess], homage is paid.

[Name of deceased priest/ess] ibaé.

(Continue until all the ancestors in the religion have been named.)

Ibaé gbogbo egun iyá mi, _____.

My respects are paid to the dead ancestors of my mother, _____ [in this blank, say your mother's full name].

Ibaé gbogbo egun babá mi, _____.

My respects are paid to all the dead ancestors of my father, _____ [in this blank, say your father's full name].

[Name of deceased family member, starting with the most recent] ibaé.

Continue naming deceased family members until all the known blood ancestors have been named in full.

Having honored creation and egun, the mojuba becomes a prayer for the protection and health of all priests and priestesses in the house at the time of consultation. Whenever a ritual of ocha is done, its energies unfold to incorporate all those who might be present, not just the diviner and client. It is hoped that the information discovered will better not just these, but also the entire *ilé ocha,* or family of orisha, of which they are a part. And even if they are not present, the diviner asks permission of his godparents and elders to proceed with the ritual, for although they are physically removed from the sacred space, the heads that gave birth to the priest are always spiritually present with him. As names are called for the blessings, those who are present for the divination will answer "Aché" to give strength to the prayer that was said for them, and to thank the diviner for their blessings.

> **Kinkanmaché iya/babá tobí mi [your godmother/ father].**
>
> **Kinkanmaché ojigbona mi [your ojigbona].**
>
> **Kinkanmaché _____ [Oluwo, godfather in Ifá].**

(*Kinkanmaché* is a phrase that asks for protection, blessings, and the good things in life. Note that in these prayers, the African name given in ocha should be used.)

> **Kinkanmaché [from here until the end, you continue with all the living godparents, grandparents in ocha, and so on of your own godparents; once that is done, you name those priests and priestesses who might be present].**
>
> **Kinkanmaché orí, eleda emi nani _____ [your own name in ocha, if ocha has been made].**
>
> **Kinkanmaché gbogbo kaleno, igboro, abure, ashire, Oluwo, iyalocha, Babalosha kale ile.**
>
> *So that nothing bad can happen to those who are present in my home: my brothers, sisters, sons, daughters, visiting priests and priestesses, priests of Ifá, the mothers, the fathers, and the keepers of the spirits who have come to my house.*

Once the mojuba is complete, it is time to call the orisha by his or her praise names and prayers. Most houses have long lists of these that they use in their ceremonies and rituals, and if an orisha has been received, the godparent will share these as they are needed. To illustrate orisha invocations, I have included some below that are nontraditional in addition to the more standard prayers. While praying, it is important that the diviner, if divining alone, begin to play the sacred instrument to focus the orisha's attention on the ceremony taking place.

For Elegguá

Eshu Elegba olo gbogbo na mirin ita algbana babá mi unlo na buruku nitosi le shonsho. Kuelu kuikuo odi. Kosí ofo; kosí ejo; kosí aro, ni oruko mi gbogbo omo nile fu kuikuo. Adupe, babá mi Elegba.

Owner of all four corners, elder of roads, my father, take all evil away, so that we can walk with plentiful health. Let there be no illness, let there be no loss, let there be no revolution, let there be no death. In the name of all the sons of this house, I thank you very much, my father Elegba.

For Ogún

Ogún agbaniye babá alagbede kuelu re le se na kife. Lai lai toni wiki nitosi gbogbo ni laye. Nitosi le onje. Olódumare ni na agbara ati, ni gbogbo na kishe bawo shishe odara ati buruku, babá Ogún mola balomi.

Great blood warrior, father warrior, with his power he does as he wishes forever. In order to kill we must say: "Warrior be able to eat." Omnipotent deity of power and of everything that is done for good or evil, Father Warrior, deity of death, take care of me.

For Obatalá

Obatalá okunrin ati obínrin ni laye eleda ni gbogbo na dara dara ati buruku oba ati ayaba, afin oga ni na bala ati gbogbo na shishe babá alaye alabo mi ati mi gbogbo na ejun, dara dara babá wa afin alano. Jekua babá mi, adupe.

Great male and female deity, world creator of all good, health, and evil, king and queen, albino owner of purity and of all justice, father who shields, grand protector of all the world, my protector and of all good and healthy things, our merciful albino father, hail, my father; thank you.

For Shangó

Shangó, babá mi, kawo ilemu fumi aleya. Tilanshani nitosi ki ko gbamu mi re oro niglati wa ibinu ki kigbo ni na orin ati gbogbo omo nijin gbodo wi kuelu kuikuo beru nitosi dilowo kawo kawo ile mi iwo bagbe babá mi ki awa na kue ni okan nitosi kunle ni iwaye ne re elese ati wi Shangó alamu oba layo ni na ile ogbe o mi.

My father, god of thunder, control my home. Give me the radiant salvation so that your word does not catch me when you are angry, you who scream in the sky. All your sons here below say with respect, and to honor you, control our homes. Remember, my father, that we call on you from our hearts, we kneel before you and ask, god of thunder, merciful king, happiness on earth, shelter us.

For Oyá

Oyá Yegbe, iya misa oyo orun, afefe iku, lelebi oke, ayagba gbogbo loya, obínrin oga mi aro, oga mi gbogbo egun, orisha ni abaya oyu ewa, Oyansan oyeri jekua, iya mi obínrin ni kuikuo le fun olugba ni Olofin nitosi wa ayagba nikua, adupe.

Oyá Yegbe, mother of day in the sky, wind of death, whirlwind from above, queen of all markets, woman owner of all spirits, owner of all illness, goddess of the marks in her pretty face, the market of the wind, who understands life, my mother, woman of great power, commanded by God to be the Queen of Death, thank you.

For Oshún

Oshún yeye mi oga, mi gbogbo ibu laye nibo, obgo mo orisha lo uwe nitosi gba ma abukon ni omi didun nitosi oni alafia ati ayo. Obínrin kuelu re aché, wiwo ati re maru asho gele nitosi yo ayaba ewa kuela re reri ati aye sugbon be toni sho nitosi ko mo nigbati wa ibinu. Obínrin iku, iko Olofin, adupe.

My mother, owner of all the rivers of the world, where all the children of the orishas go to bathe and to receive the blessing of the sweet water and to have happiness and joy. Woman with her skirt and five scarves to dance, beautiful queen with her laughter and joy, but we have to be careful because we don't know when she is angry. Woman who deals with the dead, messenger of Olófin, thank you.

For Yemayá

Yemayá orisha obínrin dudu kuele remaye, abaya mi re oyu ayaba, ano rigba oki. Mi iya mayele, oga ni gbogbo okun, yeye, omo eya lojun. Oyina ni re ta gbogbo okun nibe iwo ni re olowo nitosi re omo teriba adupe iya mi.

Black female goddess with her seven face marks, queen diviner, receive my salvation. We greet you, mother, owner of all the seas, mother, daughter of the fish. There, afar, is your throne below the sea, where you keep your riches for your obedient son. Thank you, my mother.

Having invoked the orisha, it is time to explain the reason for the divination. State for whom the question is being asked, why the question is being asked, and what the question is. Be specific, for Obí is a spirit with a limited vocabulary, and although a talented diviner can determine many things with only four pieces of coconut, if there is any vagueness in the operation, the answers received will not be specific. Once you are done with the explanation, make an offering of coconut to cool the orisha a bit, sprinkling one sliver over the orisha's vessel or image as you say each of the following three lines:

Obí n'ibi ikú.

Obí does not announce death.

Obí n'ibi arún.

Obí does not announce illness.

Obí n'ibi ofo.

Obí does not announce loss.

Each sliver sprinkled on the orisha is given as an offering to avoid death, illness, and loss. We pray to the orisha that Obí does not announce that bad things are going to happen; rather, that he will show us a way to avoid them. A final phrase is said as the remaining slivers of coconut are poured over the orisha's vessel:

Obí n'ibi araye.

Obí does not announce tragedies brought about by the world.

Again, the world is not always a safe place, and we offer a handful of coconut slivers so Obí and the orisha will have the strength to help us find a way to avoid any tragedy the world might present. Although each small slice of coconut might seem insignificant to us, the elders have said that when Elegguá takes the offering to heaven for the orishas, each small sliver again becomes whole. Having made our offerings, we finish this part of the invocation with the following words:

Kosí ikú. Kosí ofo. Kosí ano. Kosí inya. Kosí fitibo. Kosí akopa. Kosí tiya tiya. Kosí araye. Kosí gbogbowan

osogbo unlo. Fun iré owo. Iré omo. Iré arikú babáwa.

May death be no more. May loss be no more. May sickness be no more. May war be no more. May nothing be overwhelming. May nothing be disrespectful. May there be no arguments. May arguments and gossip be no more. May all misfortunes be no more. So that we may have the blessings of money. So that we may have the blessings of children. So that we may have blessings and not see death.

Having said and done these things, touch the floor with your right hand and bring it up to the coconut held in the left hand. Do this three times, saying for each motion:

Ile mokuo.

The earth is abundant.

Those who are present will respond, each time:

Akweye.

I invite you to worship.

Change the coconut now to your other hand. Make the same gesture, this time extending your hand to the orisha you are consulting and bringing it back to the coconut. Do this three times, saying each time:

[The orisha] mokuo.

[The orisha] is abundant.

Those who are present will respond, each time:

Akweye.

I invite you to worship.

Using the same hand, indicate the floor and then the coconut three times, saying:

Akweye Owo.

I invite you to worship to have money, symbolic of wellness and evolution.

Akweye omo.

I invite you to worship to have children.

Akweye arikú babáwa.

I invite you to worship so that an early death is never seen, not to encounter our immortal parents before our time.

If the coconut divination is for the self, cross and indicate the four cardinal points of the body, beginning with the head. If the coconut is for another person, touch each point of the body beginning with the head and say:

Orí inu

(the head)

Eshu ni pacuó

(the back of the neck)

Esika meji

(the shoulders)

Okokan

(the heart)

Inu

(the stomach)

Akwa meji

(the arms)

Onukun meji

(the knees)

Elese meji

(the feet)

Owo osi owo otun ono wale

(the hands)

Once these steps are complete, the diviner separates the four pieces of coconut, holding two in each hand. The white sides are pointing upward to the skies, showing the diviner's hopes and prayers for blessings and coolness in all things. The hands, palms up, are held side by side to show Olódumare that we wish to have our world in balance with no strife, no turmoil, only evolution. The two hands are circled around each other once and brought together, to show how all things must come together as one before something new and better can be created. Once all of these symbolic motions are done, the diviner lets Obí fall from waist height, giving the pieces a chance to move freely and answer well. As they are allowed to drop, the words Obíre Obí ("Coconut, for goodness, to Obí") are uttered, and all those present will respond, "Akwanya," which means "I choose to split Obí." There is only one other special rule to be followed when Obí falls for the first time during divination: If egun (an ancestral spirit) is being questioned, all women who have passed puberty yet have not passed menopause must not watch as Obí opens his first letter. The first pronouncement of the dead is not a process to be seen by women who may still bear children—the elders say that it will make a woman barren, or even cause miscarriage.

Once the coconut pieces fall on the floor, the diviner must check to see what pattern has taken shape. This first pronouncement from Obí will tell us not only if the orisha is actually present to answer our questions, but also if the orisha is pleased with us and well disposed to answering our questions. Remember that in the coconut oracle there are only five basic patterns, or letters: *alafia,* which shows four white sides; *etawa,* which shows three white sides and one dark; *ejife,* showing two white sides and two black; *okana,* which falls with three black faces and one white; and *oyekun,* showing all black rinds. If either alafia or ejife falls, the orisha is indeed present and ready to answer questions. Alafia is a throw that not only tells us the orisha is with us, but also gives his or her blessings for the divination. Ejife forebodes that this session will bring the client back into balance with his destiny. Etawa is a tricky letter if it arrives on the first fall, for it tells us the orisha is there but may not be too disposed to answering questions. Often we say, "You should not ask that which you already know." Okana is Obí's way of telling us that the orisha is not present. If this letter falls, the diviner must again begin to sound the sacred instrument of the orisha, calling him or her by all the praise names known, and perhaps by singing. If Obí answers okana again, we say that the orisha is off on important work, doing something for the diviner. At least a day should pass before the divination is done again, and perhaps an offering should be made beforehand to help draw the orisha back home.

The last letter, oyekun, can be tricky and sometimes dangerous. If it falls on the first throw, wet all four pieces with water from the *jícara* (a gourd used for libations) to cool the sign, turning each piece so that all the white rinds show. If there is a child in the house, have that child lift the pieces from the floor. Children are innocent by nature, and innocence is the quality needed to placate the heat of oyekun. When children are not present, the youngest person in the house should lift the letter from the floor. Now is the point where many ilé ocha diverge on how to handle oyekun when it comes on the first casting of Obí. Our preference is to remove oyekun from the house, casting the pieces far out into the street. Because our first pattern determines if the orisha is present and ready to speak, oyekun announces that the orisha is not willing to speak. If the client is insistent and pushes for a reading, he must be taken to the diloggún for a thorough assessment. Other houses treat Obí in oyekun as a pronouncement from the dead; for details on how to handle this, see the section on oyekun at the end of chapter 3.

Having determined that the orisha is not only present but also well disposed to answering questions, the diviner may now retrieve the oracle from the floor and begin the session. As was done during the mojuba, the diviner must address the spirit directly before his or her shrine, stating the full text of the question in a form that invites no confusion or ambiguous answers. Remember to phrase it so that the most positive response will be "Ejife," the world is in balance and all is well. Once that is done, the coconuts must be divided so that two are in each hand; the whites are to face upward (the action here is to invite all the blessings and goodness of heaven and Olódumare upon the ritual). The hands are brought apart and back together again in a wide, circular motion while the diviner says the words "Obíre *the orisha's name.*" Everyone then answers "Akwanya" as the oracle falls through the air and settles into its final pattern. The letter that is displayed marks the orisha's answer to what has been asked. The diviner records the letter, and he begins the series of rituals and prayers that will finish the interpretation of the oracle.

THREE
Interpreting the Oracle

OBÍ IS AN ORACLE containing many layers of interpretation. There are those who know it only as a simple system for obtaining yes or no answers from the orishas. Yet it comprises five basic symbols, or letters, cast when the oracle settles in a mandala formed of black and white rinds. Although these represent various degrees of yes or no answers, each of these basic patterns may also contain a variety of scientific, philosophical, religious, and metaphysical concerns, much as does the more involved oracle known as the diloggún. There are also two other overlooked principles. First, the five basic odu drawn in a single casting of Obí can demand, under the auspices of specific orishas and circumstances, a second throw that creates a meji, or double, odu. From these five signs can be drawn a total of fifteen double odu, extending the original signs of alafia, etawa, ejife, okana, and oyekun into a total of twenty letters. Each of these letters will carry its own meanings that append and extend the five parents of this oracle. Finally, the manner in which the coconut pieces fall can also mark a variety of *iré* (blessings) and *osogbo* (evil), depending on how the pieces settle in relation to each other. If the diviner has the aché, an amazing amount of material can be derived from the casting of four coconut slivers.

Our basic system of interpretation comes from the five signs that may appear when the four pieces of coconut are allowed to fall freely from the diviner's hands before the orisha petitioned. Obí will turn and twist himself as he falls humbly at both the devotee's and the orisha's feet, revealing the orisha's answer as it is known and as it relates to the basic question asked by the consultant. Remember that as Obí settles into his pattern, he will have to give an answer in one of five signs: alafia, etawa, ejife, okana, or oyekun. It is from these five basic patterns that the diviner is to begin interpreting the answers of the orishas. The full meaning of each cast will depend not only on the text of the letter that has opened, but also on the orisha being questioned and how the coconut pieces fall in relation to each other. The basic meanings of the five patterns and their meji throws (if such are indicated) follow.

alafia (four white rinds showing): Settling in a pattern that shows four white faces, Obí has brought alafia, blessings. Although in the hands of an aleyo or *santero* (priest) this oracle cannot reference odu,* the pattern itself alludes to *babá* Eji Ogbe, the first letter created by Olódumare's unfolding. It has no other possible equivalent. To show respect, the diviner must crouch low on his feet and pray, "Alafia omo. Alafia owo. Alafia Imale. Alafia ariku babáwa." In Lucumí, he has asked that alafia comes with "peace and abundance, peace manifesting with children, with prosperity, the kind of peace not seen with an

---

*To reference odu with Obí, one must visualize the coconut as an *opele* (a Babalawo's divining chain). Only priests of Ifá have this right. Their initiation, plus the prayers they use when casting the coconut, makes it possible for the Ifá priest to read the 256 odu in their session. An aleyo or santero has not the aché for this task, and even though Obí falls in a pattern mimicking odu, for him it is but an empty shell, a chance occurrence that has no meaning beyond itself. Odu cannot be invoked by those without proper initiation; it will not be present for those outside Orúnmila's priesthood. There are those who argue this point, however. As with anything else in Santería, this is an issue that must be discussed with one's godparents.

early death." Although it is a powerful mandala in the oracle, it is by no means the most positive. There are times when alafia will stand alone, answering in the affirmative; there are times when alafia will become meji, answering either yes or no. It can waver, and the diviner must be careful with his interpretation.

If Obí is being offered to Obatalá, Shangó, Yemayá, or Oshún, alafia's pattern is firm and the reading ends here; the answer to the question is yes. Although stable, however, the iré of this letter can be lost if the client does not heed the sign's advice. Here, Obatalá stands up to encourage clarity. Take no action until goals are visualized and plans firmly established. Shangó offers this pattern when he wants to warn the querent that force and strength are necessary now; however, battles must be fought defensively. Never attack. Nobility is a quality to be encouraged. Yemayá and her sister Oshún advise proper action in accordance with natural tendencies. Yemayá moves ceaselessly; her waves are relentless as they lap at the shoreline. Storms come over her, yes, but instead of being destroyed by them, they fuel her into greater action. The rivers of Oshún always flow in one direction, as should this client. They, too, are fed by life's storms; bad weather strengthens her and makes her strong. Whenever obstacles come—and they will—she rises over or around them, eventually wearing them down into her waters. For the client to know how to act in any given situation, he should look to the orishas in nature and then determine his actions.

Having opened for an orisha not considered royalty, this sign is a warning, not a firm response. Under the influence of these orishas the letter will demand that a double odu be cast to bring the oracle's closure. Elegguá, Yewá, Ogún, the Ibeyi, Ochosi, Asohano, Osain—these are examples of spirits who waver in this pattern. Under their direction, alafia comes as both a warning and a recommendation. It warns us that trials and tribulations will come, things that will throw the client off track. He may lose sight of his goals. It recommends that this person use caution, planning all actions before moving in any direction. Any thought or emotion that can "heat" the head must be stilled, for only by coolness and freshness can harm be avoided. Encourage patience. Through these orishas, alafia will never be a "yes" answer; the diviner must not assume this. It gives only the spirit's initial advice and permission to continue with the reading. Note that this sign heralds a brief period of iré, although the double letter opened may shorten its span.

When alafia demands a second casting with the orisha questioned, the following five possible combinations will mark the final pronouncements of the consultation.

alafia-meji (four white rinds followed by four white): Alafia-meji is the first set of patterns that can fall when a double odu is needed. Four solid white faces are followed by another set of four solid white faces. Remember that the oracle is cast a second time only when one questions a whimsical or variable spirit (any not considered royalty). The letter has repeated itself, and this force is emphasizing the nature of alafia. By following the advice given, a peaceful outcome is guaranteed. There is no assurance, however, that the path to attainment will be without peril. Nor does this sign promise the client exactly what is desired. Somewhere along the way, plans might change, and the orishas will provide something more essential to evolution. In alafia, the orishas promise to work for one's need, not greed. Alafia-meji is a positive omen, yet all it promises is blessings at the feet of this orisha if his or her advice is followed. Note that this is the spirit's full answer, and alafia-meji brings full closure to the oracle.

alafia-etawa (four white rinds followed by three white): Alafia-etawa is the second pattern that may be cast when a double odu is necessary. Four solid white faces are followed by a set of three light rinds and one dark. The client has come to the orishas with the unknown and is answered only by mystery. The nature of the spirit questioned is whimsical, and alafia warns us to proceed ethically, cautiously; however, the second sign given by this spirit is noncommital. Almost alafia itself, etawa shows us darkness amid the good that could be brought. Forces will seek to overcome, yet might be kept at bay by the three white rinds lying on the floor. As it is vague in its answer, the diviner needs to consider many things carefully. First, this letter could be stating that the spirit questioned cares not about the answer, nor does this orisha want to be involved. In this case, the diviner will need to petition another spirit.* Obí also could be pointing out the client's own lack of commitment. To attain his goals, he must be centered on what is important. Until the client commits to action within himself, these efforts will be wasteful. Through this sign, the orishas could be trying to say that the client is lazy. Only strong efforts will bring results. Even then, if the goal is attained, it might not be what is desired. Although not the most positive sign in this oracle, alafia-etawa ends this session with Obí; once cast, the oracle is closed.

alafia-ejife (four white rinds followed by two whites): Alafia-ejife is the third pattern one may cast when a double odu is necessary. The initial sign, alafia, is followed by a balanced mandala of two black faces and two white faces. Of all the letters in this family, only this gives a stable yes; the orisha is promising attainment. This promise is unwavering, but it is conditional on the client's actions. The advice of alafia must be followed if this person's world is to be brought into balance. Although the desired results may not come easily, they will come, and this person will have what is sought. Ending with a positive letter, the orisha speaking has brought closure to the oracle.

---

* This letter frequently falls for those who do not follow proper protocol when using Obí. It is important to use the steps given in chapter 2 for opening the oracle. In this way does the diviner determine the willingness of the orisha to answer the client's questions before they are asked.

alafia-okana (four white rinds followed by one white): Alafia-okana is the fourth pattern that may land when a meji odu is necessary. The initial sign, alafia, is followed by a mandala of one white rind and three black rinds. The diviner must advise the client as follows. First, severe difficulties will come; this person is about to enter a very volatile period in which anything negative can occur. Only with a cool, clear head can this person hope to emerge unscathed from any trial or tribulation. Second, the client must be told that the answer to his question is an unconditional no. The orisha will not change or waver in this, and no ebó will alter this person's path. Failure will be the result should these things be pursued. Only abandonment and behavior modification can prevent danger now. The diviner should note that with such a negative sign, closure cannot be assumed from the oracle. Having opened in alafia-okana, the directions in the last chapter of this book, "Closing the Session with Obí," must be followed to end this reading properly.

alafia-oyekun* (four white rinds followed by four black): Alafia-oyekun is the fifth sign that may be opened when a meji casting is necessary. Each part of this mandala is in opposition: Four white rinds are followed by four black rinds. The answer to the

---

* There are two schools of thought on how to handle a meji casting of Obí that ends in oyekun. The first method of dealing with this pattern is to treat oyekun as if it has fallen on its own; the black rinds are wet with water, turned so that all whites are showing, then ritually lifted from the floor. The diviner treats the letter as if it has fallen for the dead. For more information on this, see page 75. The second school treats each meji pattern as if it were a letter to itself. Because the pattern begins with alafia and ends with oyekun, the sign itself is alafia-oyekun and belongs to the family of alafia. It is not treated as if it were oyekun but, rather, as a pattern of alafia. If, however, the letter will not close out, the implications of the second sign must be investigated, as the dead could, quite conceivably, be standing up in this pattern for ebó. As with any information in this or any other book, consult with your religious elders before making a decision on how to handle these patterns within Obí.

question is always no; there is no way to placate or change this sign. Although the client might feel that strong effort and courageous exploration can change what the orishas have foreseen, realize that the end will bring only disappointment and failure. Following the preconceived path may even bring destruction, ruin, or death to the client. Note that when this letter falls, the diviner cannot assume closure by the oracle. He must wet the black rinds with water from the jícara, turning them over so that all the whites show. He then lifts oyekun from the floor. Now he must ask permission to close the oracle with the question "Eboda?" which translates to "Is all well [with the reading]?" The appearance of alafia, etawa, or ejife shows that the orisha has said all that needs to be said, and the oracle is closed.

If, however, okana is the answer to the diviner's question, the oracle is not closed. The orisha petitioned not only tells us that the answer is no, but also tells us that ebó is needed to keep this person from harm; the osogbo of oyekun is close. For directions on how to proceed in this circumstance, turn to chapter 5, "Closing the Session with Obí." The final sign that can come in answer to the question "Eboda?" is oyekun. Answering thus, Obí announces that there are issues to be settled with egun. Before one may address these issues, a specific set of actions must be completed to remove oyekun from the house. All four dark rinds must be oiled with red palm oil; the coconuts are then dashed liberally with water from the jícara. They are turned so that the whites of all four pieces are showing and are then put into the gourd. Finally, the youngest person in the diviner's home must take this letter outside, casting it into the street. There, the used pieces of coconut will rot, the water will evaporate, and the earth will slowly cleanse the volatile essence of oyekun. She is more than big enough to handle that task.

Having done all these things to remove oyekun from the house, Obí is opened anew using a fresh coconut. Once the oracle is prepared, the diviner, client, and others present gather before egun's shrine. The entire divination process is completed again, beginning with the prayers (mojubando) and ending with the first casting of the coconut to Obí himself. Remember, this first pattern cast determines not only if egun are present, but also if they are disposed to answering questions. Now the diviner must determine what, if anything, these spirits require, and he must phrase his question so the most positive response can be ejife, yes, the world is in balance. Because the act of mojubando is an ebó and act of worship itself (fulfilling egun's noted desire to be noticed and worshiped from the pattern of alafia-oyekun), the diviner might ask, "Are the [client's name] egun satisfied at this time?" Upon casting Obí to the floor, if alafia, etawa, or ejife comes, the spirits are satisfied. The oracle is closed; nothing more is required. It is important that the client never ignore these spirits again; to do so will hinder his evolution.

If either okana or oyekun comes, egun are not satisfied. Okana itself is a more gentle no; the client's ancestors want the darkness to dissipate before the light. Yet because they have been ignored for so long, unsatisfied by their descendant's propitiation, they have neither the strength nor the aché to help him evolve. Merely their unsatisfied presence increases this spiritual darkness. Oyekun, however, is a more dangerous no. With this mandala, we know that some of the most ancient and forgotten ancestors have come; they demand the worship and reverence that is their due. Although not working against their descendant, their presence is filled with need, with hunger, and this builds up around him as a tight, impenetrable darkness. For both okana and oyekun, the diviner must follow the material given in chapter 5's "Closing the Session with Obí." If this propitiation turns out to be fruitless (the oracle will not mark ebó or will not close off ebó), the negative letters must be oiled, watered, and taken to the street. Only an immediate session with the diloggún will settle this client's spiritual affairs.

etawa (three white rinds showing): Etawa is the second pattern that may fall when Obí is cast to an orisha. It is a mandala displaying three white sides of the coconut and one dark. The name itself is a contraction, a Lucumí phrase that means "three have come before us," the number three referring to the whites. Although light is the main power sitting before us, one dark rind is there to symbolize the impending darkness. It comes ominously, a warning to the one for whom divination has been made. There is osogbo in the letter, and this will soon be faced by the client. Forces are quickly rising to overcome, yet these are still placated by the three whites that lie on the floor. The signature itself represents a revolution coming, a subtle uprising against the iré that Obatalá and the orishas funfún (the cool orishas) could bring to this person's life. Know that while darkness tries to overwhelm the light, the light is still there. Blessings still exist, for now. Therefore, in this letter there is no implied stability—there is only strife and struggle. To help keep the darkness at bay and make this a stable omen, the diviner stands towering about the letter and prays the sacred prayer, "Etawa owo. Etawa omo. Etawa arikú babáwa. Obí kenyo!" In English, one is praying, "Etawa brings us the blessings of children, of money, of a long life [this is prayed against the uprising of darkness and with the whiteness inherent in the sign]. Obí, speak well for us!"

In almost all circumstances, the sign *etawa* will demand that the diviner once more give coconut to the orisha being petitioned. Those orishas who are considered warriors will take a second casting: Shangó, Aganyú, Ochosi, Oyá, Yewá, Ayáguna (a warrior path of Obatalá), Babaluaiye (sickness and disease are his weapons), and Elegguá will use this letter to point out an impending war. Although the war may now be silent, it will soon be fought and the client will have to struggle for the things he considers dear. Those orishas who are given to coolness and freshness will use this letter to point out the client's current state of mind. Obatalá will say that this person is not prepared to achieve much of anything. First, promote calm; second, realize that there is an inner darkness, almost a depression, rising to engulf this person. Yemayá might use etawa to show that the relentless tides of the sea are seeking to erode the stability inherent in life. Finally, Oshún shows how there will be obstructions in this person's path, and it may take awhile for her sacred waters either to wash away or to rise above these obstacles. For all these, the diviner will have to pray and retrieve the coconuts from the floor to find a more stable sign and the orisha's final pronouncements.

There are conditions under which etawa is stable, a representation of the orisha's will in relation to the client's questions. There are some orishas who do not speak through the diloggún, yet they will offer advice through Obí (they use not their own voice but instead the patterns of the orisha Obí). The Ibeyi, Ideu, Ayao, Inle, Olokun, Ainá, and Abata will give etawa as a final pronouncement. When these orishas open in this letter, they have said all they have to say and do not want to be bothered again. Ogún, who is given more to actions than to words, will complete his answer in etawa. The nature of these spirits tends toward silence, and their answers are always terse. Be advised that although to them etawa is a stable yes, it is also a conditional yes—the condition being that the client proceed with caution in all things. Finally, if one of the orishas is being questioned at his or her place in nature and etawa falls, it is then accepted as a somewhat (yet conditional) stable yes and the oracle is not thrown again. Under any other circumstances, the diviner must lift Obí from the floor and make another casting to determine the orisha's will in relation to the client's problems. Only with a double letter will stability through etawa be found.

The double letters of etawa follow.

etawa-alafia (three white rinds followed by four white): This is the first pattern that may emerge when Obí is cast twice for the orisha. Etawa is the first sign given, a mandala of one black rind and three whites, followed by alafia, a pattern of all white rinds.

Although a positive sign in the oracle, this letter does not guarantee success for the client. It marks a period of strife, struggle, and hints of unseen enemies (both within and without, psychological and physical) that will bring turmoil. The darkness will be held at bay, however, and in the end the client will receive blessings from the orishas. He may not get what he wants, but he will get something that he needs. Evolution is ensured on this path. Because this is a positive letter, Obí is closed; the orisha has said all that needs to be said.

etawa-meji (three white rinds followed by three white): This is the second pattern that may fall when Obí is cast twice for an orisha. The first sign, etawa, has repeated itself; one black rind and three white rinds has doubled. When this letter falls, it is often said that "one should not ask what is already known." The orisha petitioned is pointing out that the client already knows the answer to what has been asked, and that the spirit is not pleased about being bothered. The answer, however, is an unstable yes. Things can change as the client grows in his commitment to his evolution or loses sight of the goal. Although this is not the strongest of Obí's signs, etawa-meji does close the session. Also, the diviner should keep in mind that the sign itself also marks indifference stemming from this spirit; it is not pleased with one or more of those gathered in the room for divination.

etawa-ejife (three white rinds followed by two white): This is the third odu that can fall in this family when a meji casting is necessary. Etawa, a pattern of one dark and three white rinds, has been followed by a mandala that is balanced, two whites and two blacks. Although etawa itself wavers, ejife is the strongest pattern of all the letters; it is the most stable omen in this family. The answer to the client's question is always yes; the world will eventually be brought back into balance. The darkness uprising now in this person's life will be balanced by the light; there will be the proper mixture of the bitter and sweet;

and the client will prosper in his goals. Evolution will come—however, it may not come without a struggle. Advise this person to persevere, for the outcome will be what is desired.

etawa-okana (three white rinds followed by one white): This is the fourth pattern that can open when Obí must be cast a second time. Three white rinds are followed by three black rinds; the pattern is reversed, and it points to a reversal in the client's life. Although it always answers no to the initial question, this no is conditional. If the diviner is skilled at his work, it is possible to change the orisha's answer and find a way for the client to achieve at least part of his goals. Something important has been overlooked. Perhaps the diviner has phrased the question incorrectly. The opening statement to the orisha must be examined for flaws; it must be rephrased so that the most positive response can be made, "Yes, the world is in balance." Perhaps the client has not thought through his question clearly; he might not know what he really wants to ask. Remember that frivolity in this oracle, or unclear statements, will confuse Obí, as he has only five limited, basic signs by which to answer. With careful consideration of this letter, the divination process, and the client's issues, this letter might be changed. If an incorrect process has been used, the oracle must be put into the jícara of water and thrown into the street. A new coconut must be opened and the entire session begun again.

Because this letter does not automatically close the oracle, the diviner can, using his own aché, begin to ask a series of questions to determine what is lacking in the procedure. If the oracle gives many negative answers under continual castings, the diviner should ask permission to close the session and ponder the answers with the client. Then it should be opened with a fresh coconut to see if all will go well.

A ritual, an ebó, or even a behavioral change might be needed to bring success. These options should be checked with Obí before the oracle is asked for closure.

etawa-oyekun (three white rinds followed by four black): This is the final letter that can open in etawa's family. The initial casting of one black and three white rinds is followed by a casting of all black pieces. This is the strongest "no" of all etawa's composites, and its pronouncements are firm. Because oyekun is volatile, the diviner must complete a brief series of rituals to cool the sign. First, he crouches low to the floor and wets the dark rinds with water from the jícara. They are then turned so that all the whites are showing. Our prayer here is for peace and blessings, a prayer shown to the spirits not by words but by actions and symbols. Before speaking to the client, the diviner must rise; holding two pieces of coconut in each hand, he asks the spirit, "Eboda?" before casting Obí to the floor again. If the four rinds settle in alafia, etawa, or ejife, the oracle is closed and the diviner must deliver the following message.

"The answer to your question is no, and there is nothing that can be done to change it. Right now you walk in light, but the darkness is there and it is trying to overtake you. Continue on your present path, and it will. You will come into a period of struggle, of strife; the result will be ruin, and death (physical, emotional, mental, or spiritual) will come." This pattern does take an ebó: a *rogación* (cleansing of the head) before Obatalá. Once this is given, it is up to the client to remove himself from all who are involved with the question asked. This ebó and behavior modification are both needed to avoid osogbo now.

If okana comes as the answer to "Eboda?" the orisha petitioned is demanding ebó. Although the answer of etawa-oyekun remains unchanged, the offering prescribed here will help keep the client from danger. The diviner needs to follow the material given in chapter 5, "Closing the Session with Obí." If oyekun comes in response to "Eboda?" Obí's answers are being clouded by the dead; they are standing up for offerings and spiritual assistance. Before determining what it is they desire, oyekun must be removed from the house. Each dark sliver is oiled with *epó* (red palm oil) and refreshed with water. They are then turned so that all the white sides face upward. Having done these things, the four slices of coconut are put into the jícara of water, and the youngest person in the house casts both water and Obí into the street. Once this oyekun is removed from the house, a new coconut is opened and egun are questioned at their shrine to see what it is they want.

ejife (two white rinds showing): When the coconut's mandala is balanced, showing a series of two white rinds and two black, we know that ejife has come to the house. The orisha's answer to the client's question is simple: Yes, the world is in balance. No one piece of Obí appears out of place; no one division rises against the blessings presaged. The advice of this letter is simple: Everything the client needs for attainment and evolution is either present or coming, and cautious procession will guarantee success. The stability of this sign is lost only when the client acts foolishly or unwisely. Because this is the most positive letter in the oracle, it is closed; the orisha has said all that needs to be said. *Note:* A meji casting will never be needed for ejife.

okana (one white rind showing): Okana is the fourth pattern that may fall when Obí is cast to an orisha. The word itself, *okana,* is a Lucumí contraction that means, "we see only one" (*okán* means *one*). Before us lies a mandala of one white rind and three black. The darkness outweighs the light, overwhelming the blessings that Obatalá and the cool orishas would bring to the client's life. It is ominous, a warning that darkness and devolution are upon the client now; it cannot be ignored; it cannot be denied. Light and dark are always at war, always trying to balance and unbalance each other. Blessings still exist, minutely, yet the client is in neither a time nor a place in which they can be claimed. In this odu, we know that spiritual forces are not in proper alignment. The client has brought himself to a place in which good fortune cannot find him. Even if it did, he could not accept it. Yet just as light illuminates the end of a tunnel, the whiteness of that one light rind can lead this person through the darkness around him, and the client must be advised to look carefully for that one glimmer, that one bright star, that will take him away from all osogbo. This is a letter calling for rapid change and strong action; any force given to these things will speak in this sign. Oyá, Olokun, Ogún, Shangó, Elegguá, and Aganyú can speak here, as can the dead.

To lessen the negative effects of this pattern on both the diviner and his home, once this letter falls a short ritual must be done to cool its heated energies. The one casting Obí must first wet his fingertips with cool water. Crouching before the oracle, he then wets the dark faces of Obí and prays, "Leti okana, bata okana. Ile okana. Kosí ikú. Kosí arún. Kosí eyo. Kosí araye." This means "Listen to okana, for okana is at our feet. Okana is in our house; listen that it does not bring death, sickness, problems, or tragedies." Having offered this humble prayer, the diviner then turns over the three dark rinds so that the mandala alafia is lying before him. This series of actions shows Obí, and the orisha petitioned, that one is performing divination so that blessings can be obtained. When all these things are done, the four slices are lifted from the floor. The manner in which the divination continues depends on the reason for which it is being.

When Obí is given to an orisha before ebó is made, okana cannot always be interpreted as a refusal of, or dissatisfaction with, the sacrifice.* Remember, there are six orishas who speak strongly in this sign, as well as egun. Of these six, two always answer in the affirmative for okana: Oyá and Olokun. In this pattern, Oyá stands firm with her machete; she fights fearlessly for the client. Olokun speaks here of the darkness she loves, the peace and solitude found in the depths of the ocean. Whenever these two orishas open in okana, we consider it an affirmative answer because it assures us they are fighting the darkness on the client's behalf. For these two orishas, okana tells us that they have accepted the sacrifice as it is. The opening of okana also tells us that the aché of the offering will be used to destroy all those things standing in the way of the client's evolution. For any other type of question posed to these two spirits, it would be positive as well because okana puts the client under their spiritual protection.

The other spirits who can be said to speak through okana will have similar issues in this sign. Ogún, Shangó, Elegguá, Aganyú, and egun are all comfortable with this mandala. Unlike Olokun and Oyá, however, the diviner must ask another question to determine what these orishas are saying. Once the prayer for okana has been recited and the coconuts are lifted, the one casting should ask, "Is this okana to clear [name of client']s roads?" If the spirit then answers in alafia, etawa, or ejife, it is a good sign; the orisha has come in okana to absorb the negativity,* and the ebó being made will help the orisha with this. Etawa, however, will still signal a long, hard struggle before the client. If okana repeats itself, or if oyekun comes, something is not right with the ebó. It will absorb negativity, but something more is needed to bring it to completion. The diviner must use his own aché to figure out what might be lacking, questioning the orisha with Obí for each choice until something suitable is found. If this pattern or oyekun continues to repeat itself during this line of questioning, Obí has become heated. Okana should be removed from the house, and the entire ritual of divination must begin again using a fresh coconut.

For any orisha beyond the ones already discussed, if okana comes before making ebó, something is amiss. The diviner must contemplate what is being offered, thinking about what can be added to or taken away from the ceremony. Using his own aché and knowledge about the orisha to whom the offering is being

---

* Remembering that all questions should be phrased so that the most positive response can be made, "Yes, the world is in balance," it is assumed that the diviner has asked, "Is this ebo acceptable?" "Is everything as you wish with the ebo?" or something to that effect.

made, he must come up with elements that will complete the ebó. Each consideration must be checked by casting Obí to the orisha. Once an element is accepted, the diviner should again ask, "Eboda?" to ensure that all is well. Only when the orisha answers alafia, etawa, or ejife to this question may the ebó be considered complete.

If Obí was not cast prior to an ebó but, rather, for a question presented by a client, the diviner may continue in one of two fashions. Note that this depends on the house of ocha from which the diviner comes. Either okana is accepted at face value—it means no, and the answer to the client's question is no—or a meji pattern may be obtained to determine why the orisha is answering thus, and what may be done to alleviate the osogbo of the letter.

The double letters of okana follow.

okana-alafia (one white rind followed by four white): This is the first pattern of okana that may emerge when Obí is cast twice for the orisha. Okana was the first sign given, a mandala of one white rind and three black rinds, followed by alafia, a pattern of all white rinds (and already studied in this text). When this letter falls, the diviner should tell his client that although the goal now seems all but impossible to achieve, some attainment is possible. Now is a time of harsh energies and struggles; the tools for evolution either are not present or are hidden, and this person must work hard to acquire them. Obatalá is here, represented in okana by the one white rind that initially opened on the floor. If the client looks for the good inherent in all things and tries to let that orisha's light guide his path, in the end he will come away with blessings that are equal to or greater than that which he sought. Understand that here total success is not

---

*The nature of okana is to absorb negativity, a point that always should be kept in mind during divination.

guaranteed—life's osogbo is too harsh to give this person exactly what he wants. What this letter determines is that blessings will be found once the client has walked his path; all things will come out for the better. Note that this letter ends on a positive note, and the oracle is considered closed. The orisha has said all that is needed.

okana-etawa (one white rind and three black followed by three white and one black): This is the second pattern that may develop when Obí is cast twice for an orisha. The first sign, okana, is followed by one consisting of three white rinds and one dark; the entire mandala has given a reversal or mirror image of itself. The client's life will soon reflect this reversal of energies. The desired results of the question asked, are doubtful, however. Full attainment will not be had; the end results will be only partial, or even disappointing, to the client. Unless one has approached the orishas with a "life-altering" question, it would be wise to abandon all things connected to this. The odu predicts heartbreak, tears, and torment over the final results, and although the orishas are not forbidding a path, neither are they condoning it. When this letter falls we often say, "The ends never justify the means." Sometimes this letter warns that external negative energies can become internalized—the client could absorb what is without, turning it all into an "inner" darkness. If the client is determined to continue on this path, once his luck begins to change and the goals are partially obtained it would be wise for him to return to the orishas for a new assessment of where he is to go from that point on. Because etawa is a positive letter, the oracle is closed; the orisha has said all that it wants to say.

okana-ejife (one white rind followed by two white): This is the third sign that can open in the family of okana; the original odu of one white rind and three black rinds has been followed by a pattern that is perfectly divided and balanced. Warn the client that there are struggles and wars around him now; these are marked by the parent letter, okana. Tell him, however, that his world is being brought into balance through these things. The answer to the question asked is yes; life will once more become balanced as goals are achieved. Note that the final ejife in this pattern in no way placates the heat of the parent sign. Until the blessings are found, there will be incessant struggle. Some things, though, are worth the fight to attain them. This is the most positive sign in okana's family, and closes the reading with Obí.

okana-meji (one white rind and three black followed by one white and three black): This is the fourth pattern that may settle in this family of odu. It is a volatile sign, one that marks mounting struggles with no end or resolution. The letter is a definite no to the question asked; so severe are its energies that the diviner might wish to tell the client that the orisha consulted is forbidding any actions in connection with his question. To follow this preconceived path is to bring argument, gossip, war, treason, and destruction into the client's life. Because these energies unfold around this person now, and because the letter itself is so negative, the oracle is not closed. The one who has cast the coconut must follow the guidelines given in chapter 5, "Closing the Session with Obí." It is not uncommon for this sign to remain open until the diviner has marked one or more eboses to the orisha; the energy of okana is now open, and is slowly leading the supplicant to even more tragic osogbo.

okana-oyekun (one white rind and three black followed by four black rinds): This is the final letter that can open in the family of okana when a meji sign is needed; it is also the strongest negative answer one may receive in this series of odu. Not only is the answer to the question "no," but also the entire line of questioning must be dropped and the client must abandon those plans associated with it. The war, although it might now be silent, is being fought. Enemies are gathering (spiritual/physical, real/imagined, inward/outward) and will soon bring assault. The one glimmer of hope and enlightenment promised by okana will be lost quickly; the client will never have the chance to realize any of the blessings for which he prays. This entire letter is volatile and explosive; it must immediately be cleared from the room. The diviner must crouch low on his knees and wet the dark rinds with water from the jícara, turning over each piece until the pattern alafia shows. Only then may this sign be lifted from the floor. Because this odu is exact yet negative, the diviner must then ask the orisha if the reading can be closed. The question "Eboda?" is put to the orisha, and Obí is allowed to give a new pattern.

If alafia, etawa, or ejife comes in response to this question, the oracle is closed; the spirits have no more to say. If okana comes, the diviner must follow the guidelines given in chapter 5, "Closing the Session with Obí." If Obí gives oyekun in response to this question, there are issues stemming from the client's egun and they must be placated if the client hopes to avoid the osogbo of the letter. The sign that has fallen must be oiled: Each dark piece of rind before us is smeared with epó and then cooled with fresh water from the jícara. The rinds are turned so that all the whites show (representing our hopes for alafia, blessings) and put into the gourd of water. Finally, the youngest person in the diviner's home should take all this to the street, flinging everything as far away as possible so that the earth can consume and cleanse those energies. Having done all these things, Obí is opened anew with a fresh coconut before the diviner's egun shrine. The complete divination ritual must be done again, starting with mojubando. Once the oracle is open, the question "Are [name of client]'s egun satisfied at this time?" is put to egun. We ask the question in this manner because the most desirable response would be, "Yes, the world is in balance." If the oracle answers yes (alafia, etawa, or ejife), the prayers and attention that egun are receiving right now are enough to satisfy them. The client must be directed to pay more attention to them in the future, however, so that they never again impede his evolution. If the answer to this question is no (okana or oyekun), eboses must be marked to them until they are satisfied and the oracle can be closed. For this, follow the material in chapter 5, "Closing the Session with Obí." Even if Obí has answered in oyekun, that section's directions must be followed for marking ebó.

If this propitiation is fruitless (the oracle will not mark ebó, or will mark ebó but will not close), the negative letters are again removed from the house. Only a session with the diloggún will bring the client back into alignment, and this session must be had immediately.

oyekun (four black rinds showing): When all four pieces fall with only the black rinds exposed, we say that oyekun is in the house. In silence, the diviner crouches above the letter and wets the slices with cool water from the jícara. If there is a child in the house, he or she must be called to lift oyekun from the floor; children are innocent, and only innocence may placate this sign.* All four pieces of Obí are turned so the whites show, and then they are lifted from the floor. Having opened in a mandala of darkness, we know not only that the answer to the client's question is no, but also that something is amiss spiritually. Before continuing, the diviner must determine why oyekun has come. If oyekun comes repeatedly during this investigation, the pieces are not only wet with water from the jícara, but they also must be put into the gourd. Oyekun is taken out into the street and flung as far the house as possible. New pieces must be cut from a fresh coconut, and the session begins anew.

Oyekun's implications can be harsh; the amount of ritual attention it receives helps to reduce its severity. Through it, we find those spirits who preside over the most mysterious regions of land and sea, orishas who partake of both life and death. Yewá, Oba, Oyá, Babaluaiye, Odua, orisha Oko, Aganyú, and Olokun are all

---

* If there is no child in the house, the diviner must perform all these actions himself.

found here. If one of these is being consulted when oyekun falls, the implications of the pattern are dire indeed. Generally, this letter presages immediate death, unforeseen problems, tragedy, revolution, and bad news. There will be battles and uncontrollable anger among those for whom it has fallen. If the diviner is skillful, however, Obí can show us how to avoid what oyekun brings. Once Obí is retrieved from the floor, the diviner should begin his questioning by determining if oyekun represents the orisha's full answer to the client. He must ask, "Eboda?" Followed by alafia, etawa, or ejife, oyekun has come only as a stern pronouncement from the orisha questioned. The oracle is closed, and the diviner may begin to advise his client based on this.

If the answer to "Eboda?" is either okana or oyekun, the pattern remains open and must be marked and placated. Know that oyekun can arrive for another beyond the client: The diviner, or even someone else in the room at the time of oyekun's falling, can be marked for its influence. First we must determine for whom this letter speaks. The first question the diviner should ask is, "[orisha's name], does this oyekun fall for [client's name]?" If Obí answers no, the diviner must ask if oyekun is for himself. Obí again answering no, the diviner must ask this question for each person present. If all possibilities are exhausted and oyekun still remains unmarked, the diviner may ask, "Are egun demanding ebó?" If the answer to this is yes, the spirits supporting the entire house are in need of offerings. Before egun's shrine, using fresh coconuts, the diviner must mark ebó. If, however, the diviner has come this far in his questioning and all answers have been negative, Obí is heated. Oyekun or okana must be oiled, watered, and taken from the house. A new coconut is opened for this session, and if the new patterns that fall are calmer, oyekun is indeed gone from the house and all is well.

If the diviner can mark oyekun on a specific person, the next question to ask is, "Are [person's name] egun standing up for ebó?" One tries to mark this sign on the needs of the dead, for the primary meaning of oyekun is death. Consisting of darkness, one's dead come through that darkness, known and forgotten, to claim their respect and offerings. If Obí answers yes to this question, the diviner must now determine their needs by careful, diligent questioning. Ebó must be marked following the guidelines in the "Marking Ebó with Obí" section of chapter 5. For egun, it is important that the diviner begin with cool, simple things, slowly working his way up to the more involved eboses. Once something has been marked, the diviner must ask, "Ke ebofin ke eboda?" which means "Has the sacrifice that has been offered been accepted?" If so, the coconuts are disposed of to remove their heat from the house and new coconuts are opened so that the client's original concerns may be addressed.*

Finally, if oyekun falls on a person and the diviner determines that the dead are not speaking, or if after the dead speak oyekun returns frequently, there are serious spiritual forces at work that must be cleared from this client. The letter must be oiled, watered, and removed from the house. The diviner should advise the client, "Oyekun marks death, traps, treason, and cataclysmic change. Its letter is hot, and this heat is entering your life. It must be fought." As soon as possible, this client must have a session with the diloggún to find the reasons for oyekun's visit. Only in this way can the sign be cleared.

A special note on this letter: Once the pattern has been closed and cleared from the house, if it has fallen repeatedly, or if there have been many negative answers in the session, everyone in the room should call home immediately or call a neighbor to check his home. Oyekun sometimes, for reasons unknown, marks unexpected fires, accidents, and tragedies in the home, even if the letter fell for someone or something else. Those who have left young children or the

---

* Two things must be noted here. Even if oyekun fell from the dead, many houses still take that sign as a "No" answer to the client's original concerns. I do not. If the sign fell for the dead, or for another in the room, how can it also answer the client's question? Also, if the dead interrupt the second session as well, something is spiritually amiss; the client must sit immediately with the diloggún.

elderly at home should be especially worried—but why would any-one leave a young child or elderly person at home alone?

Additional Considerations on the Five Basic Patterns

The manner in which the five basic patterns fall contains a wealth of information on the question asked, and the diviner should keep these omens in mind:

☗ Occasionally one or more of the white pieces will fall touching each other, and there are also times when they will be partially, or entirely, piled one on top of the other. When this happens, Obí predicts good fortune (iré) for the client, and although most diviners consider this iré to be financial, there is no limit to the type of iré marked by Obí. If only two pieces fall this way, this shows general blessings; three or four, however, indicate that a surprise will soon manifest. The connected pieces should be reverently lifted from the floor and the client should be directed to kiss each one. They are then put into his cupped hands and the diviner instructs the client to put both hands into his pockets to seal the iré, making it firm.

☗ If a black side falls on top of a white side, something is blocking the individual's good fortune, perhaps uncon-scious sorcery or evil magic. When the reverse occurs—one white side falls on top of one black rind—there will be misfortune hidden behind the blessing that is proph-esied in the pattern.

☗ If two or more black rinds mount one another, it seals death, treason, traps, and witchcraft. These, even if they are only two in ejife, should be wet with water from the jícara and then separated on the floor before they are lifted. This simple ritual helps to destroy the obstacles the client will face.

❦ When a piece of coconut falls on its edge and does not show a single side, the diviner reads the letter according to which part of the coconut faces him: white or black. However, it is said that the dead are claiming something from this reading or offering, or perhaps interrupting the ceremony. The diviner must next investigate what the dead are trying to do. If the coconuts fall on their edges throughout the reading, it is possible that either his or the client's egun are trying to alert the diviner to fraudulent claims or danger from the client. The reading must be handled with caution and quickly brought to a close.

❦ During divination, especially when Obí is responding well, if a piece of coconut breaks off, this is given to the client to place in the purse or pocket for twenty-four hours as a charm. It is an omen of good luck, and the client takes this energy with him once the reading is over. If part of a black rind breaks off and lands up white, the same is done, for it shows the client will take away something good from the struggle. If a piece of a black rind breaks off and still shows its black rind, it is an omen of ill luck. The black piece should be wet with water from the jícara, turned to show the white side, and then thrown to the street to remove the impending osogbo.

FOUR

Interpreting the Oracle: Apere Ti, Obí

THE INTERPRETATION OF FIVE LETTERS and their composites is the first step in unraveling the answers of Obí. For most questions brought to the orishas through this oracle, those patterns alone will suffice. Many will offer Obí before an adimú or ebó is placed before a shrine; others will question their spirits before making minor decisions that could affect their lives in subtle ways. The twenty letters based on alafia, etawa, ejife, okana, and oyekun are sufficient for these things. There are times, however, when one petitions an orisha for more serious concerns, and there are those who consult their orishas through this medium because they have neither the knowledge nor the skill to carry out the more meticulous manipulations of the oracle known as the diloggún.

Apere Ti, Obí

When the questions presented through coconut divination become more complex, however, or when the basic patterns seem too cryptic, there is another form of interpretation known as *apere ti, Obí*.* The word *apere* means "symbol," and alludes to the geometric designs that may be found in a single casting of coconuts. Note that while all the orishas may be given Obí, the aperes are used only when petitioning Elegguá. In Santeriá, just as his diloggún is most frequently consulted by diviners, so does the art of apere belong exclusively to him.

When marking an apere before Elegguá, the diviner looks closely at the first casting given for the client's question. Once the four coconut pieces have settled, one of ten possible patterns has fallen. Note that apere will not open for all readings. While Elegguá must answer the question asked with one of five signs (alafia, etawa, ejife, okana, or oyekun), an apere comes only if another orisha wishes to advise the client on his or her issues. If an apere is found in Obí's pattern, the diviner must mark it by calling out its name. For example, if Okana has fallen before Elegguá, but the coconuts land in Ogún's apere, the diviner should announce, "Okana apere Ogún," to seal in the sign. Note, too, that if a meji casting of Obí is needed to complete a session, apere may not be marked on the second casting of coconuts. A true apere can open only for the first pattern thrown. Keeping these rules in mind, the ten aperes and their meanings with each letter of Obí follow.

Apere in Elegguá

Figure 1. Apere Elegguá
Elegguá's apere appears when all four coconut slivers form a horizontal line between the orisha and the diviner.

alafia: When the first casting of Obí comes in alafia and rests in Elegguá's apere, the orisha is offering peace and reassurance to

---

* A good translation of this phrase would be, "your symbol, Obí."

the client. No matter the concerns that brought this person before the orishas, the path on which he travels is one of evolution. Although fortune has wavered drastically, all that this client has experienced has brought him to this one moment, and it is a moment that will change the course of his life for the better. Presently, the orí is clear; it is neither too heated nor too cool. Any obstacles now can be surmounted by clear thought and calm action; counsel this person to make sure that his goals are clearly delineated and well planned. The advice of alafia is the key to continual evolution, and because Elegguá normally demands a second casting, the advice of this letter is the key to locking in iré. If the pattern completing this meji is a negative sign, in Elegguá's apere it points out that this person is on the verge of losing his iré—his head will get too hot and he will not act calmly or rationally. Take the completing patterns of okana or oyekun as a warning and prescribe a rogación as a way of keeping the orí cool and refreshed.

The client should also be told that alafia apere Elegguá promises many visitors to the home. Most of these will come uninvited, but the one for whom Obí was cast will feel the need to invite others. When entertaining, this person should listen more than he speaks. Someone will bring important news, and others will identify sources of treason and despair in his life.

There is an ebó that comes with this apere. Every Friday evening, a tall, clear glass should be filled with equal amounts of water and rum. An inverted saucer is placed over this and, holding the two together firmly, they are turned upside down. This should be placed behind the front door. On top of the inverted glass, a white candle should be melted to the surface. While blowing clouds of cigar smoke over this ebó, the client should pray to Elegguá that he protect the home and all who live in it. Saturday morning, after the candle has burnt out, the remnants of the cigar and the liquid into the glass should be thrown into the street. Anything sent to the client (gossip, treason, negative energies) will be absorbed into this glass, and the earth will recycle it into something good.

etawa: This apere will never be complete without a second casting. When it falls, Elegguá is reprimanding the client, but mildly. Darkness is threatening, and although it is still overwhelmed by the light, the light itself may soon abandon this person (the meji sign will determine the full implications). Revolutions and uprisings might come, and one's stability could be lost. Apere Elegguá in etawa tells us this is because the client's plans are not complete, nor are his goals well visualized. This person needs seclusion to rest, to think. He must develop his goals firmly and then plan how to attain them. This letter also marks a spiritually impoverished person whose poverty manifests as sloth and untidiness in the house.

The ebó to correct these things is complex. First, the house must be thoroughly cleaned. Even dust should be removed from the corners of the dwelling. A pure, clean home uplifts the soul. Once this person's house is clean, it must never be allowed to fall into disarray again. To do so is to invite the orisha's anger; remember, in this religion the home is our temple. Finally, a rogación should be given at the feet of the godparent's orisha after the house is clean. This will strengthen the client's defenses while he finds his path to evolution.

ejife: In Obí, we say that ejife is Elegguá's true home. Before us lies a balance of white and black rinds: light and dark, mystery and revelation, life and death, ancestors and descendants. The world stands in balance before the orisha who creates that balance. Apere Elegguá in ejife demands specific considerations, however. The orisha is answering yes to the client's initial questioning, but goes beyond that to flag particular concerns. Although all is well now, the orisha's intervention through apere warns that intrigue, strife, and danger could manifest from beyond the client's environment. He warns, "Be cautious in all new things." For the next month or so, this person must not venture into any unfamiliar places unless the unfamiliar deals with the issue brought to Elegguá. Do not stray outdoors too early in the morning or too late at night. Do not drive down unknown roads or venture into unknown neighborhoods. Stay away from places that have not been visited before; now is not the time for a vacation or a business trip. Strangers should be avoided, and nothing new beyond present issues should be begun. Only in this way will the iré of the sign stay with the client.

There are eboses that must be done in this pattern. Before the client takes leave of Eshu, the diviner must make three brown packets, each containing toasted corn, *jutía* (a bush rat), and smoked fish. The client is then directed to cleanse himself from head to toe with each, putting them in Elegguá's clay dish. This cleansing is quite simple: the client rubs the brown packets briskly over his entire body, making sure that no appendage goes untouched. The diviner then presses the coconut pieces to the client's heart while offering a prayer to Eshu. The coconut pieces are placed back on the floor before the orisha, again displaying the sign of ejife. The next day, an adimú consisting of fresh *ñame* (yam) must be put to him, along with five green bananas or plantains that have been smeared with honey. A *derecho* (ritual fee) of $3.21 should be left with the diviner, as it is his Elegguá to whom ebó is made. Once this adimú has been placed, the brown packets and the four pieces of coconut are lifted from the floor and taken to a crossroads. The client will then have Elegguá's protection from the osogbos marked in this letter. Note that the bananas should remain with Elegguá until they begin to turn brown; the ñame stays with him indefinitely. A vine might begin to grow from this; it is a sign of growing iré. If the root rots, however, it should be removed and another must be given to the orisha. Elegguá is using the ebó to absorb negativity.

okana: When okana comes in Elegguá's apere, it can be an omen of good or ill fortune, depending on the letter that completes it. Remember that although okana itself is negative, its aché is to absorb negativity. The diviner must cast a meji sign; only in this way can okana's full influence be assessed. Looking at just this apere, however, one may make several inferences about its meanings. The client has entered a period of swift change at Eshu's feet. Now he is surrounded by darkness, yet there is that one powerful spark of light. Should the client focus on that light, that one glimmer of hope, his fortune will be reversed. Elegguá is, after all, a spirit of reversal. The dead are here as well; the client's own egun whisper from the darkness. They warn him away from it and toward the light, but they know of their descendant's curiosity. He will be tempted to wander into darkness, to seek the faces behind the voices. This will cause his downfall. The diviner must tell his client to propitiate egun at their shrine once every day, but no more than that. A prohibition must be prescribed as well: If he hears his name called out from behind, he must walk away from that voice and not turn to see who it is. Thus will he walk away from danger.

If the composite cast from okana ends in alafia, etawa, or ejife, the client's life will improve. The light will dominate, and he will enjoy some degree of success in his affairs. This depends on the exact composite opened; the diviner must study the letter so that nothing is missed. If either okana or oyekun completes this casting, success is not guaranteed. The diviner must follow the meanings and rituals of these signs carefully. No matter what opens beyond this apere, there are several things that must be kept in mind to help this person avoid osogbo. The diviner must tell the client that he is surrounded by those who wear two faces. One face is of the friend whom he knows, but the other is of a total stranger, someone evil and vile who wishes the client's downfall. Jealousy abounds, and Elegguá says to trust no one until he has proved himself. He assures the client that he has the aché to tell truth from falsehood, and he must use it. Okana apere Elegguá also marks witchcraft or bad luck at one's front door; this should be kept in mind.

This pattern also takes ebó: A young rooster must be fed to Elegguá. One week after the sacrifice, an adimú of cool fruits should be given to refresh the orisha. If the client does not have Elegguá, he is now marked for the reception of the warriors, and this ebó should be done immediately to the diviner's orishas.

oyekun: Oyekun apere Elegguá is a volatile sign; it is hot and must be handled with care. There are issues between the client and his godparents in ocha: A chasm, some great divide, has arisen between them and Elegguá says it must be healed. There are issues between this person and his egun; they clamor for attention and must be given a series of three *misas* (masses, seances) so their needs and desires may be explored. There are issues with Elegguá as well; if the client does not have him, he must receive him, and if he is already in the client's life, he must be fed a rooster. This is why oyekun has fallen in this apere, and until the eboses prescribed are complete, Elegguá will not comment on the client's concerns. Even the crowing orisha has grown weary of this child, but to explore this the client must have a session with the diloggún as soon as possible. The diviner should note that with all this person's protections unsettled, the client is in continual danger. These issues must be cleared up as soon as possible.

Apere in Ogún

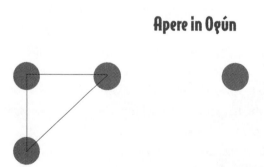

Figure 2. Apere Ogún
Ogún's apere appears when three pieces of coconut form an isosceles triangle in which one angle is 90 degrees and the other two are 45 degrees each and one piece of coconut lies outside the perimeter of that triangle.

alafia: This pattern is a paradox. When it falls before Elegguá in Ogún's apere, the diviner knows that the client's life up to this moment has been filled with strife and turmoil. He may be exhausted; he does not sleep well and worries over things that he cannot control. At times this person can be exceedingly lazy, yet it is laziness born of the desire to rest, maybe even to give up. Then there are times when the client fights and works hard, but a previous lack of initiative has made many of his obstacles insurmountable. The orishas know how hard this person has worked. They know his dreams and desires. Ogún, the proud, fierce warrior who never rests, stands before this person's side. He offers his help, his strength, and his advice. In alafia, that advice is simple. The diviner should tell the client, "You have Elegguá's blessings. You have Ogún's blessings. But now you must focus on what it is you want. You must continue to work hard, but pace yourself. Remember that there is no recovery from total exhaustion."

This pattern, however, is not a complete answer. With Ogún's help it can presage eventual success. Ogún is here to warn the client that he must be cautious in his dealings. But cowardice and fear must never be mistaken for caution. Ogún says not to be afraid, for he will stand by this person's side and will fight all his battles. To him an ebó of seven cigars and seven small, single-serving-size bottles of rum must be placed. Daily for seven days Ogún must be sprayed with one bottle of rum; he is then given a single cigar. This will lock in the iré of this sign. Because a composite must be opened here, either Okana or Oyekun may come. If Okana is the final sign in this reading, Elegguá is telling the client that the answer to the question asked is no, but Ogún (if ebó is made) will open alternative opportunities and keep this person from harm. If Oyekun completes the composite, the answer is still no. Egun must be given adimú, and the client's plans must be changed. Together, Ogún and egun will work to bring new opportunities, replacing what has been denied.

etawa: Opening with this apere in etawa, Ogún says that light is being threatened by darkness. Although the white rinds do outnumber the black, that darkness is thick, almost impenetrable, and almost upon the client. Blessings are trying to come, yet they are held back. Ogún says the client's thoughts are not good; he is overlooking something important and this will be his downfall. Ogún says the client is trying too hard, using too much force, and this should have been his first clue that something was amiss. Ogún says to open the eyes: Intrigue and treason stand before the client. A silent war is being fought among friends. Many with whom the person associates do not have his best interests in mind. To come out of this pattern unscathed, ebó must be made to the warriors. Together Ogún and Elegguá must be fed a rooster, and then the client should have a rogación. This will help clear the osogbo of this sign. The orisha's final responses to the question asked will be made clear when the composite is thrown.

ejife: This letter always answers, "Yes, all is well," but when it opens in Ogún's apere, he comes to offer advice and to mark an ebó that will seal in this iré for good. First, Ogún says that the answer to this client's question should have been apparent from the start. If this person were to put all his faith in the orishas, thinking more about them and not about secular activities, his entire life would come into balance. He warns of women and gossip—do not gossip with them, and do not trust any woman with secrets. In time, a woman will tell all that the client has said. As ebó to seal in the iré of this letter, put a large basket of cool fruits (nothing red) to the warriors for seven days. After this, leave the ebó to Elegguá and Ogún in the woods (it would be best to pick a lonely spot of railroad tracks in the woods to dispose of this ebó). If travel beyond the client's city becomes a necessity during the next twenty-one days, he should make this ebó to the warriors again so the trip will go well. Ogún also gives a stern warning: Be cautious when going to the four corners or crossing the street. There could be danger.

okana: When Elegguá gives okana in Ogún's apere, it is a bad omen. Darkness is overwhelming, yet the one white rind gives a meager glimmer of hope, a chance to overcome adversity if the client acts wisely. Ogún is fierce in this letter, almost angry, and the supplicant's egun stand behind this orisha to support his actions. Ogún comes with his apere to tell the client others are wishing him ill on a daily basis, and although deliberate witch-craft is not being sent, the force of these combined thoughts equals the power of a spell. This person's mouth, pride, and vanity have caused these things. Soon his head must be cleansed with a rooster, and this animal is then fed to the warriors.* Once done, a rogación should be given before their shrine. Only in this way will his head have the strength to fight. The following day all these items should be left at a railroad with a derecho of twenty-one cents. *Note:* It is imperative to follow the traditional line of questioning for okana when this apere opens; more eboses may be needed to keep the client from harm.

oyekun: When oyekun falls before Elegguá in Ogún's apere, it falls on the client. The diviner does not need to mark the reason for its appearance. Tell the supplicant the following things. Ogún is standing up to defend him, but in the end, only Olófin will keep him from death. Death is near in this sign; the client is in very real danger. Do not fight. Do not argue. Do not carry weapons or travel with those who do. Be cautious of open flames and electrical devices. Do not go out at night, and do not be on the streets at three, seven, or nine in the afternoon and evening.

---

* To cleanse the head with a rooster or with any other item, the cleans-ing object is touched to the head and gently circled around it many times. It is believed that doing so transmits any negative energy to the item used for the cleansing.

Immediately, cleanse the head with a white pigeon, feeding this to Ogún; follow this ebó with a rogación. Finally, as soon as possible this person should sit with the diloggún for a more thorough assessment. Note that none of these concerns stems from the client's initial question. They come because this energy is around him and needs to be resolved. Once these warnings are given, the sign should be removed from the house; a new coconut must be opened to address the client's original concerns. Ogún has interrupted the original casting to warn this person of things he did not know.

Apere in Ochosi

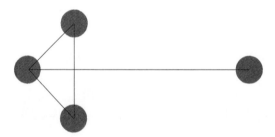

Figure 3. Apere Ochosi
Ochosi's apere is formed when three pieces of coconut form an equilateral triangle, with one coconut piece forming a straight line with one of the angles. This cuts one leg of the triangle in half, and the resulting figure mimics the form of an arrow.

alafia: Having opened before Eshu in alafia apere Ochosi, the reading has taken an interesting turn. Elegguá gives his blessings; he offers guidance and hope for the client's concerns. Normally an unstable pattern, when manifesting in Ochosi's apere this letter stands firm; not only is the client well focused on his goals, but he knows how to attain them as well. One must wonder why advice is being sought when success is imminent. Even though alafia is firm here, the rules of Obí demand a second casting. If the client truly believes in himself and in his work, this pattern will be followed by either alafia or ejife. Doubting himself, etawa will open. If either okana or oyekun comes after alafia apere Ochosi, the client is at war within himself, and any eboses marked by Obí will help settle this war. For these two patterns, it is imperative that the diviner assure his client, "Elegguá gives you his blessings; he opens the roads to success. And you have Ochosi guiding you toward your true destiny. How can things go wrong? You must believe in yourself and put your trust in the orishas. There is no other way!"

It is good that the client has Ochosi as his guide, for false paths are open in the world. At this time, however, the client walks properly. He must stay this way. Alafia apere Ochosi does warn that as he progresses, there will be distractions; and he could be led astray when he begins to doubt himself. Ochosi wants this person to focus on three things now: the orisha, the goal, and himself. Others will try to give advice; do not listen. Ochosi says that, for now, there are enemies. The things the client seeks will harm false friends as they are attained. They know this. The client knew this even before the oracle was opened. He should never forget it.

This sign does take an ebó. A single seven-day candle should be given to each of the warriors in his favorite color. To Ochosi, an extra adimú must be given: a bottle of anisette.

etawa: Before Elegguá lies a pattern of three white rinds and one dark; etawa has come to the house. Normally a sign announcing struggle and revolution, in Ochosi's apere it is an omen of danger. Light is all around the client, but it is to his back as he walks into darkness. Blessings do exist, but this person is in neither a time nor a place in which goodness may be claimed, for while he began his journey with a clear, delineated goal, somewhere along the way he lost sight of it all and has walked into danger. This apere tells the diviner that Ochosi is near; the supplicant has his strength and protection at his disposal. Depending on the meji sign cast from etawa, he may well need it. If alafia or etawa comes after this, success is not guaranteed, even with Ochosi's help. One has his blessings to continue, and something good will come at the end of the struggle; however, the end will not be what was sought. Okana and oyekun bring disaster and despair, and before this session ends the client may have many eboses to make. Only ejife can bring evolution, and that is contingent on the client's understanding of all the orishas have said he can or cannot do; he must heed the advice of this reading in order to evolve.

This sign does have its ebó. All the warriors must be given adimú, and special consideration should be given to Ochosi. Once every four months, the client must also have a rogación to keep his head clear from osogbo.

ejife: Ejife apere Ochosi is a favorable omen for most; it is a symbol of balance not unlike the scales of justice for which Ochosi is known. For those who are noble and law abiding, this is a pattern of fulfillment. One reaps what one has sown. Yet not all who open in this apere will be noble and just people, and when Ochosi speaks to these in ejife, it is an omen of bad tidings. Before giving any advice for this apere, the diviner must ask, "Are you living outside the law? Are you doing anything now that could bring you into the court system?" If the client answers yes, know that Ochosi may soon bring punishment; however, it will not be unfair considering what this person has done. If the client can answer honestly that he lives within the law, Ochosi has brought a blessing. To seal in the iré of this sign, the client must make ebó: adimú at the feet of Ochosi. After he has been appeased, all the warriors must be given something together. If the client does not have his warriors, this is done to the diviner's orishas, and the client must receive his warriors soon.

okana: When Elegguá gives okana in Ochosi's apere, it is a bad omen. The three dark rinds that sit on the floor before us mark desperation, enemies, and ill fortune. The light is still there, one single white rind standing alone against these things. It is not enough, however, to overcome the darkness that overwhelms. The dead stand behind this as well, the client's ancestors who have been all but forgotten, and they come almost in anger. Their lack of prayers and offerings is part of their anger, but it arises more from this person's not living up to his potential. He does not use the gifts bestowed on him as part of his spiritual and genetic heritage. If the client faces court hearings or arrest due to illegal activities, this sign becomes even more harsh, for Ochosi is not happy; he is not yet angry, but he stands over this person like a disappointed parent considering what punishment to give. To open roads that have been closed in this apere, the client must return to the diviner's home as soon as possible with a rooster for Elegguá; he must be cleansed with this, and then it is sacrificed to that orisha. After this sacrifice, Ochosi must be fed as well. Make sure that one week after the sacrifice is offered, both orishas are given baskets of cool fruits as refreshment, and Ochosi must be given an adimú of something sweet to change his feelings toward this client. All these things will be in vain, however, unless the client practices behavior modification and alters those things that wrought Ochosi's anger. Ochosi is justice, and can be appeased only so much before he will render judgment.

oyekun: Sitting before Elegguá in Ochosi's apere, this pattern speaks of death, the dead, and darkness. Ochosi says that most of this person's problems are brought by the dead, and he comes to show the client how to move through and beyond this darkness. First, egun must have what they want: ebó. To them this client should offer a rooster; if he has not the *opá ikú* (staff of the dead), he should go out in the woods with his godparent to find one. Immediately, it should be fed. A series of misas are then offered to this person's ancestors; three should be given on three consecutive nights after the opá has been fed to egun. Immediately after the final misa, the client's head should be fed a single white pigeon before Ochosi's shrine, giving the orí the strength it needs to travel the path laid out by this orisha. After it is fed, the client should have a rogación before that orisha's shrine. With egun satisfied and strengthened, and with the head fed and calm, the client will be able to look at his life with refreshed vigor; he will be able to overcome those things that hold him back from evolution.

Apere in Babaluaiye

Figure 4. Apere Babaluaiye
Babaluaiye's apere appears when three pieces of coconut form a relatively straight line, with one piece above and outside the upper left side or upper right side of the line.

alafia: When Babaluaiye's apere appears before Elegguá, alafia is its most desired odu. Here we say that Asohano loves this client, and such is his love that his messengers—mosquitoes and dogs—will feel the orisha all around him. During the day, dogs will come to him with much love and affection; they are Babaluaiye's constant, dependable companions and will want to be closer to that spirit by being closer to the client. These vibrations are also felt by the orisha's nighttime companions, mosquitoes, and the client should not venture out too much after dark lest he be swarmed by these as well.

This letter warns against putting faith in plaster and paper; if this person has accumulated religious icons in these mediums, they should be destroyed. Do not throw them away or give them to another, because the osogbo of having them will extend to the new owner. Remember: Even though we thank the saints for helping us preserve our religion, our devotion goes to the orishas and not to the icons of our captors.

Alafia apere Babaluaiye marks this person for the orisha's reception. Until this can be done, the client should make ebó to the orisha and receive his eleke. In this sign, he takes an ear of roasted corn smeared with epó; it is to be given with a small loaf of bread. If this apere comes for one who has Babaluaiye, the orisha feels that he is too close to a door. He wants to be hidden from view in a quiet corner of the house.

etawa: When Babaluaiye's apere appears before Elegguá in etawa, it is a warning. The client takes too many medicines for both real and imagined symptoms. This must stop unless he is under a physician's care. Many illnesses are minor, and they are avenues for the body to cleanse itself with Asohano's help. To take things that reduce symptoms while illness runs its course (which is what almost all over-the-counter remedies do) is to reduce the body's chance to cleanse itself and heal naturally. Remember that those things that do not kill us only serve to make us stronger. Also, consider that when one reduces an illness's symptom without proper medical intervention, the diagnosis of more serious diseases can be missed. If the client is not currently taking over-the-counter remedies, this apere in Asohano warns him that when he becomes ill again, he is to go straight to a physician and take nothing that is not prescribed by a doctor.

This pattern has its ebó to help the client overcome any osogbo: He must wear sackcloth underwear under his clothing every day for seventeen days, and at the end of this period he should give Asohano an adimú (anything that his heart dictates will be acceptable).

ejife: While Elegguá gives this as a yes answer to the client's concerns, showing that his world is in balance, Asohano intervenes with his apere to deliver a very important message. This client is born to be a priest or priestess, and if the crowning orisha has not been determined, it may well be he. Even if this is not the case, Babaluaiye loves this client dearly and wants to be more involved in his life. As soon as possible, the client should commit to receiving this orisha. He will work miracle after miracle in his life. Also, consider that this person may have ancestors who were initiated to the orishas or involved deeply in orisha worship. The ancestral background of this client should be investigated; a genealogical chart should be drawn up, and those egun should be loved, adored, and propitiated on a continual basis.

okana: When okana opens before Elegguá in Babaluaiye's apere, it is a stern warning, yet one given out of love. This orisha smiles down on the client; he watches over him constantly. Okana is deep, dark, and mysterious, and those orishas who know the dark depths of human existence can be found in this sign. With Babaluaiye, this odu not only warns but also absorbs: The orisha can remove all the blockages from this person's path if he heeds the advice this spirit is giving. First, Asohano demands, not begs, that the client speak more gently of himself and others. Profanity must never escape his lips, not even as a whisper, and this person should blaspheme no more. This goes not only for the religion of the orishas, the Lucumí faith, but also for the religions of other people. Tell the client this: "There is truth to all paths that preach goodness; even if the followers themselves cannot find that truth and goodness, it is still there. Do not curse the light lest you find yourself alone in darkness."

The client is prideful, vain, and slothful at times, and these are qualities that feed the darkness. Yet within there is still the desire to be good, to do good, and to have good things through hard work; this is what brings the one white rind and the tiny spark of light that can grow if it is nurtured.

As ebó, this person must wear the *elekes* (beaded necklaces) of the cool orishas daily. If they are not had, they must be received: Obatalá, Yemayá, Oshún, and Shangó must accompany him at all times. This person should also have a rogación before this orisha's shrine, and he should contemplate the spirit's lessons of humility before he is allowed to leave the diviner's home.

oyekun: Oyekun is a dangerous sign in itself, but when it opens before Elegguá in Babaluaiye's apere, it is even more severe. This client is in danger of death; disease is coming, creeping up on him slowly, and could even be brewing inside his chest right now. The letter oyekun must be placated as described in chapter 3; the reason for its falling must be investigated. As soon as this oracle is closed, those things marked by egun and Obí must be fulfilled immediately.

The fact that this odu has fallen also marks several eboses that should be done by the client to honor Babaluaiye. First, this person must wear sackcloth and "beggar's clothing" from time to time; he should go out into the street to beg alms, and must give all money that he receives to a true person in need. Once this is done, a bowl of cool fruits should be given to all the warriors and Babaluaiye should be offered a rooster. With this rooster the client must be cleansed head to toe, and then it is to be offered to the orisha. Because sickness is so close to this person, he should begin saving money to make ocha. In time, that initiation will become his salvation.

Apere in Aganyú

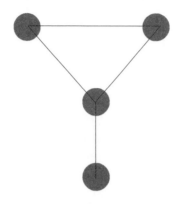

Figure 5. Apere Aganyú

Aganyú's apere appears when an equilateral triangle is formed by three slices, with one slice forming a straight line with one of the angles of the triangle. This line formed by the errant piece of coconut and an angle does not intersect any line of the triangle; it remains outside the figure.

alafia: When this apere opens before Elegguá in alafia, Aganyú has stood up in the reading to caution and advise the client. First, the one who brought issues to the orishas is timid and shy; if he is loud and boisterous on the outside, it is only a mask he wears. Yet he does not wear it well, for when overwhelmed by others he quickly retreats back into himself. To this person, Aganyú says, "Do not be timid! Be proud!" This information should be relayed to the client. The orisha is strong, powerful, and masculine, and his energy follows this person through his current journeys. As long as the client pays attention to him, all things will come out well. Because much spiritual heat follows Aganyú wherever he treads, the client must guard his head, making sure that it does not become overwhelmed or over-heated. He should also be cautioned against overworking himself to the point of exhaustion, for the spiritual currents that propel him forward are fierce indeed. As ebó, it is important that this client cleanse his head frequently with two coconuts; once that is done, they should be put to Aganyú so he takes the heat and not this person. If it is obvious that the client is overwhelmed, a rogación should be given before Aganyú's shrine. This way, the spirit does not overwhelm the client as he seeks to help him on his journey.

etawa: Here, Aganyú comes to say that the client is having difficulties because he does not walk a straight path to his goals. He begins to work toward one thing, and as he walks his path this person easily becomes distracted by things on either side of it. Wandering, he gets lost before he once again starts working toward his goal. This is what the darkness of etawa tells us. The solution to this is simple: Concentrate on one thing at a time. The composite letter that opens will tell the diviner how well the client will do this; it also tells us if there are other things impeding progress, and if this goal should be abandoned altogether for something new. Etawa apere Aganyú also recommends that this client seek out the advice of his elders on all his life's goals; many of the things that he seeks, they have sought, and their advice will help him achieve without misfortune.

As ebó, this letter marks that a rooster be given first to the warriors, and then adimú should be left to Aganyú's shrine to thank him for his help and advice.

ejife: Although ejife is the most positive sign of Obí, answering yes to the client's concerns, when it opens in Aganyú's apere it flags issues that must be addressed. The diviner should assess the client's relationship with Ogún. He should ask, "How do you relate to your Ogún? Do you pray to him frequently?" This apere tells us that the client petitions Ogún more than he should; this is a powerful orisha who works hard, but prefers to work alone. The diviner should impress on his client not to bother Ogún for anything, that this orisha knows his needs and will take care of them. Instead, this person must focus on Elegguá first and Aganyú second; they are the ones who will take care of the things that Ogún cannot or will not.

This sign does not prescribe a specific ebó; however, to ensure Aganyú's goodwill, an adimú should be given "from the heart." As the client gives to the orisha out of love, so shall Aganyú give to the client out of love.

okana: Having opened in Aganyú's apere, the diviner knows the reason for the darkness around the client. Before Elegguá, okana apere Aganyú marks the war of the sexes. Here, women cause problems for men and men go out of their way to cause problems for women; the opposite sex cannot be trusted to have one's best interests in mind. If the client has superiors of the opposite sex, this makes his life all the more difficult. To overcome these things, the client's life needs to go through some drastic changes. The answer to his question is no; he cannot succeed. Yet if he changes his goals just a bit, he might still come out ahead. This, of course, depends on him keeping his own counsel. Dreams and desires must not be discussed with others.

Note that while Aganyú speaks in this apere, it is Elegguá who needs to be given ebó. The sacrifice of a rooster to Eshu will do much to clear the client's paths from osogbo.

oyekun: In this pattern of apere Aganyú, it is he who delivers the warning, but egun and Obatalá are the ones who take ebó. The orisha stands before Elegguá to deliver a stern admonition: Make fun of no one, especially the infirm and the elderly. Obatalá once came to this client in disguise, riding on one of his legitimate but uninitiated children, and in that guise the client offended the orisha. This is why his things are not going well; this is why he cannot evolve. Aganyú stands here to deliver this warning because Obatalá himself is too offended to give it himself, and will not speak to the client or work for his benefit until ebó is made and forgiveness sought.

First, ebó must go to egun. They have not been properly propitiated, and they demand adimú before they will let the client go before the orishas again. Once this is done, the client must be cleansed with a white pigeon, which is then fed to Obatalá. A second white pigeon is fed to the orisha to placate him, and a rogación must be had before his shrine. After being cleansed, the client should pay foribale to the orisha and beg his forgiveness, promising never to taunt anyone who is old, infirm, or deformed. To do so after completing these eboses will cut off his roads to evolution permanently.

Apere in Shangó

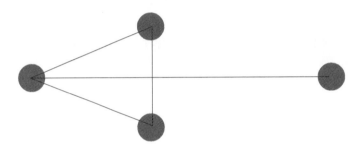

Figure 6. Apere Shangó
Apere Shangó appears when three coconut slices form a tight isosceles triangle, with one coconut forming a straight line with the apex of the sharpest angle. The resuling figure mimics a sword, which Shangó uses in his battles.

alafia: Although alafia is always a good omen, when it opens before Elegguá in Shangó's apere it is a strong announcement of the thunder god's pleasure. The mighty Shangó has watched this client closely, guarding him from harm and leading him gently on his path to evolution. Always helpful but never interfering, Shangó has studied how this person conducts himself. He knows the client's innermost thoughts. Shangó is impressed with what he has seen. The diviner should say, "You have brought your concerns before Elegguá, but it is Shangó who has answered you. This orisha has been close, watching over you and guarding you, but he has never interfered in your actions. He is very pleased with your goals, your ideals, and your methods of attainment. Shangó is with you. He gives you his blessings. As long as you continue to live for what is right, Shangó will help you evolve." The diviner should also tell the client that hisothers more than he will ever know; he should always consider this in all that he does or says. The important life choices he makes will reverberate far beyond his immediate environment.

Alafia apere Shangó takes an ebó. As soon as possible, the client should return with a large basket of cool, fresh fruits. He is to cleanse himself with these, putting half to Shangó and half to Obatalá. Once done, both orishas will continue to bless all that this person does in life.

etawa: When this apere falls before Elegguá in etawa, Shangó comes to say that the client's foundations are not as strong as they should be. The orisha wants to help, however, but first the client will need to make at least three eboses to clear his paths. First, the client must bring Shangó a bunch of green plantains. Each of these must be greased liberally with red palm oil and then placed on a white plate with a red border. Over these a large amount of honey should be freely poured. The diviner places this offering over Shangó's *batea* (tureen) while the client pays foribale to the orisha, praying for the strength and evolution required. At the end of this, a red candle and a white candle are lit to Shangó. Having made his ebó, the diviner should now seat the client for a rogación; once done, using Obí, the diviner should ask the orisha where the remains of both the rogación and the ebó are to be taken. The following morning, the matter used to cleanse the head is taken to that location, and when the plantains start to turn brown, the client must take those to the same place as well. Coming to remove this offering, a new white ceramic horse tied in red ribbon should be brought to the diviner's orisha; this is left in place of the plantains. When these things have been done, Shangó will fight to clear the aborisha's paths.

ejife: When ejife apere Shangó opens before Elegguá, there can be no greater assurance that all is as it should be in the supplicant's life. Shangó has come with Eshu to reassure that all is well; the world is coming into balance, and the client has all the tools for evolution. This does not mean that all will be sweetness and love, however. Rather, ejife promises a perfect balance of light and dark, sweetness and bitterness, evolution and destruction. This balance of opposite forces is what creates evolution; it is what drives us to become something better.

Ejife apere Shangó does take ebó: The client must give the orisha a beaded, wooden sword. This is presented to him with a small adimú of plantains. Once Shangó has his sword, he will make sure that no enemy can harm this person in his pursuit of happiness.

okana: Although normally a poor omen, when okana apere Shangó opens before Elegguá, the letter shines with hope and freedom if the client carefully heeds the orisha's words. The diviner must tell the client, "While you may see light and hope all around you, in truth there is only darkness; but Shangó comes offering help. Unknown to you, doors are closing and paths are overgrown; your evolution is blocked. Shangó can save you. Only he can light the way." Each dark rind lying before the diviner represents a single friend and the treason this friend would bring. Note that these are not enemies, nor do they mean to be. The influence of those around the client brings unintentional harm; they are innocent of their actions, yet are to blame for the turmoil coming the client's way. The diviner should impress on this person, "Your goals, your plans, your dreams—

these do not go well because others always interfere. Your dreams will take you away from those who love you, and they want to keep you close. This is the real reason they interfere without meaning to hold you down. Focus, for now, on Shangó."

It is he who will lead the client to victory, he who will remove the osogbo of false friends so that this person may attain his goals. And once he has achieved them, those who are truly his friends will still be there, waiting. They will understand, and will forgive him for having temporarily removed himself from their circle. The advice of this letter is simple: Make plans and keep them secret. Tell your friends that you are very busy, and then distance yourself from them while you work to evolve. Tell no one about this reading; just let Shangó lead the way.

This sign takes a few eboses to clear the client's paths, and these must be done soon. First, the diviner must cleanse the client with a small rooster, feeding it to both Elegguá and Ogún. This is followed with a cleansing by pigeon, and it is fed to Ogún only. After these things are done, an adimú should be given to shangó consisting of two coconuts, twelve candles, honey, coconut oil, cascarilla (an aromatic shrub), a wooden sword, and $6.25. Once all these things are complete, the mighty Shangó will hold the darkness at bay while the client works hard for his evolution.

Note that the composite letter cast for this sign tells whether the client will continue to evolve. If a negative pattern follows this, it shows that the client will fail because of his own disbelief.

oyekun: Oyekun in Shangó's apere is a dire warning: the client's environment is volatile, spiritually heated, and soon this heat could manifest as fire. There are many things that must be done when this pattern has fallen on the mat, and all must be treated as ebó. First, broken appliances must not be used; anything that does not work properly must be thrown out immediately. Things with frayed cords must not be used until those cords are replaced, and if they cannot be replaced, these must be discarded as well. It is possible that much of this heat comes to the client in the form of too much electricity in the home, so have no more than one appliance plugged into an outlet at any time. Extension cords are taboo: They bring Shangó's fire too far into the home. Once these issues have been addressed, the client must clean his home thoroughly, removing all trash and unwanted papers. Finally, once the home is clean and broken appliances are removed, this person should return to Shangó with an adimú of cool fruits.

Having told the client all these things, the diviner must now follow the normal pattern of questioning for oyekun as detailed in chapter 3.

Apere in Obatalá

Figure 7. Apere Obatalá
Obatalá's apere appears when the four pieces of coconut fall into a figure suggestive of a parallelogram.

alafia: When Obatalá's apere opens before Elegguá in alafia, it comes to prescribe a series of taboos and eboses that will ensure that the blessings of alafia are not missed by the client. The diviner should tell this person several things. First, the head is large and must be made to ocha: The orishas are waiting for this client to be crowned, and until this happens, true happiness will not be found. Dirt and filth are to be avoided in this client's life; he should clean himself, his home, and his car, making sure that they stay clean. The home must be a quiet refuge from life, and fights or arguments should not be permitted there. He should limit his visitors to his closest friends, and must not entertain too frequently. Food that is cooked with firewood must not be consumed, even if inside a rotisserie restaurant. White beans, pigeons, and white foods must not be consumed. These belong only to Obatalá, and he is taking these away from the client for now. Cats and dogs are also taboo, and if there are none living in this person's house, he must not take in any. Bad luck will come with them.

In this apere, the orisha wants the client to know that he hears all his prayers; Obatalá always listens and watches. Yet he needs several eboses if this person wants the orisha to continue working for him. First, because the head is so big, it must be cleansed and kept that way. The diviner should make a rogacíon to this person's head monthly until ocha is made. After the rogación is done, the client should be cleaned head to toe with two white coconuts, and these are put to the orisha with two white candles. Frequent cleansings are important to this client, and he must be taught how to do several before leaving the diviner's house. White is beautiful; it should be worn more often, and the client should wear Obatalá's eleke frequently. The diviner also directs this person to adore the warriors daily, and if he does not have them, he must receive them. Finally, because gossip and evil tongues follow this person, he should make ebó with a cow's tongue to Shangó. He shows the ebó first to Obatalá, and then leaves it with Shangó. Shangó will fight all this client's battles and keep evil tongues from hurting him.

etawa: Having opened before Elegguá in Obatalá's apere, this pattern warns the client of impending disaster, turmoil that will be held at bay by Obatalá if only the client listens. Right now, this person's life seems good and stable, but darkness is coming, an osogbo seeking to overturn the iré that Obatalá would give. This period of devolution threatens because the client has not thought through all his actions: He sees his goals, he works for them, yet he does not pay attention to the path that he walks. It is as if he has on blinders. Although Obatalá has stood up to tell the client these things, it is to the warriors that the supplicant must turn now for help. Elegguá, Ogún, Ochosi, and Ósun are the ones who will keeps his path clear while the mighty Obatalá fights to bring blessings to his life.

First, if the client does not have the warriors, he must receive them. Second, if the client does not have the warriors, the diviner's orishas must be fed two pigeons and two roosters so that they have the strength to fight this person's battles. One week after the sacrifice is made, a small basket of fruits must be given to the warriors to refresh them.

Note that if the client has the warriors, this ebó is done to his orishas: Elegguá, Ogún, Ochosi, and Ósun are fed together. If the client does not have the warriors, before receiving these spirits the sacrifice must be made to the diviner's orishas. His Ósun, however, is not fed. The pigeon that would go to Ósun goes to the aborisha's head instead, and then he must have a rogación before Obatalá's shrine. Only if all these things are done will the client have the strength to continue on his path.

ejife: Obatalá is balance, ejife is balance. When this apere opens before Elegguá, Obatalá has come to say that he is pleased with the client. All roads and paths to evolution are clear; the head is clean and the soul is pure. The orisha stands proudly over this person, blessing his life's goals so that, in time, all things can be attained. Such is this orisha's love that whenever there is a special request, it should be made with an adimú and Obatalá will move heaven and earth to make is so.

This pattern also offers an ebó that the client may use whenever he is confused or overwhelmed. With two fresh coconuts, the client must cleanse his head. He then puts these to the orisha with two white candles. Obatalá will lift the turmoil and confusion so that the aborisha may see things as they truly are.

okana: With Obatalá's apere sitting before Elegguá in okana, the cool orisha has brought a warning: Life is entering a volatile pattern, a period in which all hope and love can be lost from this person's life. He stands strong here, however, and works fiercely like a warrior to bring back light into this person's life. The client must stand strong and work hard to overcome adversity. Because he is surrounded by so much hypocrisy, this client must trust no one, not even his best friend. Reserve is called for, and the client must not speak of his plans, goals, dreams, and desires to others. The cause of okana in this person's life is simple: His own indiscretion has brought his osogbo. His own overly trusting nature has paved the roads to destruction. To Obatalá should be put a ñame with the client's name inside on brown paper; this must be covered heavily with *efun* (a chalk made of powdered eggshell). It is given to the orisha on a white plate, and the vine allowed to grow freely until the root starts to rot. Thus will Obatalá help this person grow and overcome the evil that exists around him.

oyekun: Although oyekun is never a good omen, when Obatalá speaks through this pattern it is dire indeed. He has come to tell the client that he walks in a valley of darkness, of death; all around is evil, and even the dead have come to confuse him. The client may feel he is a victim of circumstance, but the truth is that he has brought these things on himself. To impress on him the severity of this sign, the diviner must say, "Oyekun has opened in Obatalá's apere; neither he, Elegguá, nor the dead are pleased. Through your own carelessness and lack of insight, you have walked a path that has brought you into total darkness. Now the light is so far away that you cannot see it. Just as you have brought yourself to this place, so must you work to bring yourself out of it. The spirits have not abandoned you, although it feels that they have. Rather, you have abandoned them, and you must work hard to bring them back into your life.

First, the client's head needs strength to overcome the

darkness, to see clearly where vision is all but impossible. Before Obatalá's shrine, this client must sit, dressed in white, and there he should have a rogación. When this ebó is done, the diviner must not be surprised if Obí's letters do not come out well. After the rogación, the client should give an adimú to the orisha (anything his heart desires), and he must return nightly for a rogación until both Obatalá and Eshu ni pacuó both agree that the head is good again. Only the signs of alafia or ejife may be accepted as their approval. When these signs are obtained, two white doves or white pigeons should be offered to Obatalá in thanks.

This client's egun must also be given sacrifice at their shrine, and nightly the client should hold some sort of mass for them. At the end of each mass, Obí should be offered to egun. Until they show their pleasure or acceptance through either alafia or ejife, the mass must be repeated again the next evening.

Once Obatalá and egun are satisfied, the warriors must be fed two roosters and two pigeons. Elegguá, Ogún, Ochosi, and Ósun will need the strength of a sacrifice to make clear agaion the client's roads. If the aborisha does not have the warriors, this is done to the diviner's spirits; however, the diviner's Ósun is not fed. Instead, the pigeon is used to feed the client's head and another rogación is given before Obatalá's shrine.

Apere in Oyá

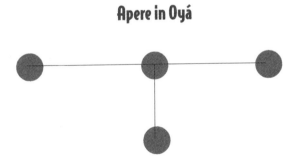

Figure 8. Apere Oyá
Oyá's apere is formed when three pieces of coconut form a straight line, and the fourth forms an intersecting line with the central piece.

alafia: When alafia apere Oyá opens before Elegguá, the blessings are great indeed, for Elegguá is fate and destiny; it is with his assay that all things in heaven and on earth are possible. Just as he wields great power, so too does Oyá. She is the lady of the market. It is there that the merchant can become rich and the consumer sated. The world, in our faith, is the marketplace, and it is Oyá who rules supreme. With blessings from her and with blessings from Eshu, there is nothing in this life that cannot be accomplished. Elegguá bends fate to the client's desires, while Oyá teaches this person how to be both merchant and consumer. With such a powerful combination, nothing can be denied. Yet although the lady of the market stands up for this person, so do the armies of the dead, which are hers to command. Vast spiritual forces have gathered to bring this client to the light.

Blessings come in this sign, but Oyá still has much advice to give. To keep the luck that she would bring, this person must not make promises. Life will soon be chaotic: There are many changes coming, and what the client thought he could do for others will be impossible. Promises are to be made infrequently, and never promise to do anything big. At work, errors will be made. This person tends to hide his mistakes, and Oyá says this is wrong. Instead of hiding them, he must point them out, apologize, and work harder to correct them. Those in power will be pleased.

Alafia apere Oyá does take an ebó. To refresh himself, the client must draw a cool bath. Into this he should sprinkle the petals of nine flowers, all of different colors. After bathing, he must dress in white and cover his head with a hat. Just before sunrise or just before sunset, still dressed in white, the client should go to the poorest, oldest, most forgotten cemetery he can find. Asking Oyá's permission at the gate, he should wander until he feels drawn to a grave; there he is to leave a bouquet of nine different-colored flowers. Back at the gate, this person should pour his heart out to Oyá before leaving. She will hear and bless his requests.

etawa: Having come in apere Oyá, etawa is a pattern marking darkness and despair. The light is in power; blessings are trying to come. Goodness does exist around this person, but he can focus only on the darkness. The diviner should look carefully at the client: This person wears a mask. His face might appear pleasant, hopeful, even happy—but beneath that are tears and turmoil. This person is depressed, and he hides it from the world. It is said that the eyes are the mirror to the soul, and if the diviner would only look into this person's eyes, he would see how tired he is. Insomnia plagues this person at night, and when sleep does come it is fitful and filled with surreal images and nightmares. Oyá says that these things come because the client works too hard, pushing himself to exhaustion; he worries too much, and about things over which he has no control. All this the client must let go. Both Oyá and Elegguá want to help, but the supplicant is in neither a time nor a place in which blessings might be claimed.

As ebó in this apere, the client must have a rogación every week for nine weeks. It is to be done before Oyá's shrine, and the diviner must mark nine items to be used in it. This will help him rest better, and the client will be able to focus on what is most important. Note that if he does not heed the advice of the reading, he will fail miserably in spite of this ebó.

ejife: Ejife apere Oyá before Elegguá is a pattern whose advice is split. Before Elegguá, this answers yes to the client's original concern. He has brought himself to a time and a place in which balance exists and all things are possible. Yet Oyá intercepts all this; she is disappointed in the client. When the advice is heeded, however, this person's fortune will change for the good.

In short, Oyá is not happy. All that this person possesses comes from her; she has been the foundation in his life. Egun support the client as well, yet they do not get the recognition they deserve. The client is afraid of Oyá and the dead souls that accompany her; she is not pleased. Bringing love and support, she is met in fear, and this person has little to fear from the mighty queen. One of Oyá's gifts is to bring swift, rapid change. The diviner should tell the client, "Think about the many changes that you have gone through in your life: They were swift, severe, and tumultuous, yet the end result of each brought you greater iré. The old was torn down to build the new. This is the work of Oyá! Never again are you to meet those changes with fear. Thank Oyá for the blessings that she brings." Also, note that the client has much aché with dreams. Regarding this, the diviner should say, "While you sleep, you have many important dreams that you do not remember later. Some of these frighten you when they are remembered. They are from Oyá and the dead. She warns you of death so you do not end up as one of the dead before your time. Heed those dreams."

This pattern has its ebó. The client must sew a *pañuelo* (handkerchief) for Oyá using nine colors; the base color must be burgundy, and it should be highlighted with eight other colors. Adorn the cloth with many cowries. When it is complete, it should be brought to the diviner's Oyá with a bouquet of multicolored flowers. The client's head is cleansed with the pañuelo; once it covers Oyá, she will remove the last remaining vestiges of osogbo. The flowers are given to her as a votive adimú.

okana: In itself, okana is never a good omen; it is a pattern in which darkness overwhelms the light, and although the light is still there, it is weak. It is ominous, a warning that darkness and devolution are on the client now. Yet okana can bring evolution, but the client will have to work hard. He will have to heed what the orishas have to say. Here it is Oyá who speaks, and she knows the danger that okana can bring. This osogbo comes from neither the client nor his actions; it comes from the bad intentions of others. If the evil presaged by okana is to be avoided, for the next three months this person must live in all but seclusion. He must keep to himself, seeking his own company and counsel. During this time, several special invitations to social gatherings may arrive. Oyá forbids their attendance. Do not go with a group to restaurants, theaters, malls, or parties. They will be filled with gossip, treason, and bad intentions. Because okana is heavily dependent on a meji casting when it opens before Elegguá, the final pattern will determine how well the client adheres to this. It will also give Elegguá's final answer to the question asked.

Okana apere Oyá takes ebó. Before leaving the diviner's house, the supplicant must be cleansed with a coconut. It is then put in a basket and left under running water until the client is gone. This person must take nine baths at home; they are to be done on nine consecutive nights with nine herbs of Oyá, and to the bathwater itself must be added petals from nine different-colored flowers. At the end of each bath, he should cleanse himself with a fresh coconut, putting this to his Elegguá.

oyekun: Oyekun apere Oyá is very specific as to the reason that oyekun has come: This client is plagued by an evil spirit, an egun that is not his, and it must be removed. This spirit has either been sent to the client or has attached itself to him because the client went somewhere that he should not have been; no matter why he has it, it must be removed. As soon as Obí has given closure, the client must have a rogación with nine things before Oyá's shrine. His head must have the strength to stay clean in spite of this sending. His own egun must be strengthened with a series of nine misas, and any prescription given by the *espiritistas* (mediums) must be followed exactly. After the ninth misa, the client must have another rogación before Oyá, and is then cleansed head to toe with a white pigeon. Allowed to fly free from the diviner's front door, this pigeon will carry away the evil spirit to heaven, where it will be dealt with for good. The day after this, white flowers should be placed in every room of the client's house to keep it clean.

Apere in Oshún

Figure 9. Apere Oshún
Apere Oshún appears when the four pieces of coconut
fall into a pattern suggesting a curve.

alafia: Alafia is a sign that brings blessings, and when it opens before Elegguá in Oshún's apere it is, perhaps, the most beautiful of all patterns. Those who know Oshún know her as the youngest of all Olódumare's creations. She is also the sweetest and among the most powerful of the spirits. Love, truth, beauty, prosperity, and sweetness are all hers to give, and when blessed by Oshún, an aborisha has within his grasp everything that makes life worth living. The diviner should tell the client, "Before Elegguá, you have blessings, and he says that these come from Oshún. *Maferefún* [Praise be to] Oshún, for she is the one spirit who can make life worth living. In this pattern she loves you, and soon your life will reflect that love. Honor her, worship her, and she will shower you with many blessings." Life now may be rough and things might be bitter, but Oshún guarantees that if the client flows steadfast like the river, he will continue to evolve, rising above all obstacles.

To honor this queen, the aborisha should make the ebó of this sign. With the most expensive yellow silks or satins he can afford, the client should sew a pañuelo for Oshún with his own hands. As he adorns this with white lace and cowries, each stitch should be a prayer in praise of the orisha. Once the cloth is complete, the aborisha should return to the diviner's Oshún, presenting it to her with two coconuts and two white candles. Before her shrine, the diviner must cleanse the client with the pañuelo; once it covers her sopera, Oshún will remove the last vestiges of osogbo from this person's life. Lighting the two white candles to her, the client should pray for his evolution. He will then know her love, as all hindrances in his life will be removed and replaced with sweetness.

etawa: When Oshún's apere appears before Elegguá in etawa, it has all the same meanings and considerations as alafia; however, something or someone in the client's life is not right, and darkness threatens to overwhelm this person. Oshún does not want this to happen, but the client must make several eboses if she is to help him. First, the ebó of alafia apere Oshún must be done, but with the pañuelo the client should bring a small gourd, smoked fish, jutía, honey, toasted corn, two coconuts, and two white candles. The coconuts and candles should be presented on a white plate with a derecho for the diviner. All these extra items except the coconuts and candles are mixed together in the gourd, and are then presented to Oshún. The diviner cleans the client's head with the pañuelo, then gives him a rogación before Oshún. The following morning the items remaining on the client's head are removed and put into the gourd, and all are taken to Oshún at the river. On the banks, the client should then pray to this queen for all the good things life has to offer. With hard work and perseverance, they will come.

There are two other eboses that must be done by the client when etawa apere Oshún comes. First, a wooden ladder with fifteen rungs should be purchased in Oshún's name. This is kept just inside the client's front door, leaning against the wall. With this ebó, Oshún will help the supplicant climb the ladder to success. Next, a white pillow with a yellow swan should be sewn for each bed, sofa, and chair in the house. This will bring luck to the client, and all who visit him will be amiable during their stay.

ejife: When ejife apere Oshún opens before Elegguá, this beautiful queen has come to announce her pleasure with the client. He has brought himself to a time and a place where there is balance. Life is becoming the perfect mixture of sweetness and bitterness, happiness and sadness, euphoria and melancholy. Although this person may not realize it, he has all the things that make life worth living, and he should thank Oshún for her many blessings.

Having answered in this apere, Oshún should be offered the following eboses. A bolt of yellow cloth should be presented to Oshún. This is left with her for five days. If the client is a woman, at the end of this time enough material is taken from that bolt to make five yellow slips or five pairs of underwear. Once sewn, these should be worn daily for luck. Also, an adimú of five honey cakes and five cool fruits must be given to Oshún as soon as possible. This will seal in the iré of the pattern.

okana: Having opened in okana apere Oshún, the orisha is coming to reprimand the client. She wants this person to evolve; she wants him to have and enjoy all the sweetness that life has to offer. The client does not live well, however, and no matter how hard Oshún works to bring him light, he surrounds himself with darkness. The diviner must be stern with the client, telling him, "Oshún wants to bless you, but your life is such that you cannot receive blessings. She says you spend too much time worrying. You come up with bad ideas, and you try to act on these. You contemplate vile, evil things, and you sink yourself in self-doubt and worry. Oshún tells you to focus on the good, not the bad. You need to spend less time questioning and more time doing. Only in this way can you hope to overcome adversity."

There is one ebó in this apere that must be done to lift its osogbo. Before Oshún's shrine, the client's head must be cleansed with a white pigeon. This is then fed to Oshún. After the cleansing, the diviner must give the client a rogación.

oyekun: Having fallen in Oshún's apere, in oyekun this orisha is displaying mild anger with the client. The diviner should tell this person, "For many years, Oshún has been with you. She has brought you much of what you desire although she got little in return. Now she demands payment; she demands ebó." The pañuelo from alafia apere Oshún must be made, and the aborisha must prepare a crown for his orisha. If this is an aleyo who has not made ocha, he must still do these things for the diviner's Oshún. If the diviner's Oshún already has a pañuelo and crown, the new pañuelo and crown must be finer that what she already has. Note that here the dead can be standing up as well, and the diviner must mark what it is they require before the reading will close successfully.

Apere in Yemayá

Figure 10. Apere Yemayá
Apere Yemayá has opened when the four pieces of coconut fall into a
pattern suggestive of an ocean wave.

alafia: Opening before Elegguá in Yemayá's apere, this pattern is both a blessing and a warning. It is a blessing because both orishas come now to give their love, their advice, and their help. Alafia requires a double casting before Elegguá. Although the meji sign determines Obí's final answer, no matter the pronouncements the iré given by these spirits cannot be taken away; it is their gift. Yet Yemayá has much to tell this person, and the diviner must say, "Once, your aspirations were pure, your heart was good, and your intentions noble. This is why Yemayá loves you so. Yet you have begun to change, and she wants you as you were. She says to stand back. Look at the big picture and how you affect all around you. Yemayá warns you not to become hard and selfish. No matter what happens to you, remain kind and loving. Be aware of how your life affects the lives around you. Do this, and she will always love you, and she will move heaven and earth to help you evolve."

As ebó in this pattern, the client must take seven baths on seven consecutive nights using seven of Yemayá's herbs. He should present a basket of fresh fruits to her at the diviner's shrine, and give a basket of fruit to the ocean. Thus will he continue to evolve in life.

etawa: When this apere opens in etawa before Elegguá, Yemayá has intercepted the reading to tell the client not only that is darkness coming, but also whence that darkness comes. The single black rind facing the diviner represents not an energy or even an issue but, rather, a person, perhaps a close friend, who will bring treason and disaster to this person's front door. In etawa, even one's friends can become enemies. Before ending this session, it is imperative that both the diviner and the client determine who this enemy is. If it becomes apparent that the client has no enemies, it must be discovered who will unwittingly betray him. This person must not be allowed into the client's house for twenty-one days, and if possible, this person must be avoided on the streets at all costs if the supplicant hopes to hold the osogbo of this sign at bay. In this apere, there are also unpaid debts to Yemayá, and these must be made good on as soon as possible. If the client cannot remember owing anything to this orisha, an ebó must be marked with Obí before the session can be ended.

In addition to what Obí marks as ebó, this apere brings three considerations that must be fulfilled by the client as soon as possible. Blue gingham should be worn daily to honor Yemayá. It is up to the client how he wants to wear this, but it must be worn even if only as an undergarment. An adimú must be given to this orisha immediately: seven balls of *gofio* (cornmeal) made with sweet molasses. It is to stay with Yemayá for seven days, and if possible taken to the ocean once it is removed from her shrine. Also, the client should hide a lodestone somewhere in his home; it will bring luck.

ejife: When Yemayá's pattern opens before Elegguá in ejife, it brings great blessings. If the client's life does not yet reflect balance, it soon will. He has worked hard, and hard work rarely goes unrewarded. In thanks for his blessings, an adimú should be brought to Yemayá's feet. Thus will iré continue to grow.

okana: When okana lies before Elegguá in Yemayá's apere, it is a dire warning: Osogbo and darkness lurk on this path. There are so close that they are all but unavoidable. Lies, treason, gossip, separation—all these could be coming. Yemayá warns the client to hold tightly to those he considers dear. Family, friends, and lovers could quarrel. Ebó must be made quickly. The warriors are to be given a rooster, and Yemayá must be fed as well. After this, her eleke is to be worn daily for seven days, and the client should cleanse himself in the ocean.

oyekun: When oyekun settles before Elegguá in Yemayá's apere, it signals several things. First, this is a person who has many questions, and the one presented to Elegguá touches only the surface of what boils beneath. The diviner should remind the client that Obí is a limited oracle, and to answer all the questions the supplicant should be taken to the diloggún for a session so that the orishas may speak more clearly about his life. The dead present themselves here as well, but instead of hindering or warning the client, they come to offer help. That aid does not come without a price, however. A series of seven spiritual misas, one per week, should be offered in the client's home so that they can monitor and advise. After the last misa is given, the client should return to the diviner's home. There he is cleansed before the warriors. Use coconut, smoked fish, jutía, and toasted corn. He should be cleansed with a white pigeon as well. Everything except the pigeon goes to the warriors. The pigeon should be set free out the diviner's front door.

FIVE
Closing the Session with Obí

OBÍ'S SYSTEM IS UNIQUE among oracles: It is designed so that a session will end with a positive letter, some sort of blessing ensuring that help has been received. Having cast the coconuts, if the answer to the client's concerns ends with alafia, etawa, or ejife, the session has closed. No further questioning is needed, as Obí has brought blessings. If the orisha ended his final pattern with either okana or oyekun, one may not assume that the session has closed. Of themselves, these patterns do not bring iré, yet careful work with them can ensure that the client receive spiritual help. Something bad can give birth to something good if only the client will listen to what has been said. The diviner must retrieve the four pieces of coconut from the floor, turning them so that the whites face upward. With two in each hand, he must ask the orisha "Eboda?" which means, "Is all well [with the reading]?" The pieces are cast to the floor and allowed to settle in a new pattern. If alafia, etawa, or ejife comes, the diviner says, "*Modupue* [orisha's name]!" which means "Thank you." He crosses his arms over his chest, then uncrosses them so he may kiss his fingertips. Touching the floor now with the fingers of both hands completes the ritual considerations for this session.

If either okana or oyekun comes in answer to "Eboda?" one knows there are more issues that must be settled. The sign falling gives clues as to what might be amiss. Oyekun is the pattern dealing with death and the dead; remember that it speaks of darkness and one's forgotten ancestors. Also keep in mind that some orishas—Yewá, Oyá, Oba, Babaluaiye, Odua, Aganyú, Orisha Oko, and Olokun—feel at ease in this letter's darkness. Any of these spirits, even egun, could stand up now to claim ebó before the sign closes. Okana, however, has issues different from those of oyekun. Being a mandala of one white rind amid three black, this symbol whispers that there is a blessing still to be claimed. First, something must be done to overcome the osogbo of the three dark rinds. Keep in mind, though, that certain spirits call this pattern home, and thus are comfortable in its energies: Oyá, Olokun, Ogún, Shangó, Elegguá, and Aganyú may all dwell in its mandala. Even the dead can speak here; any of these might claim ebó once okana has fallen.

To determine what is needed, the diviner should use the following list of questions as a guide to completing the session with Obí. Although some diviners might feel otherwise, for these questions it is not necessary to cast a composite odu. The patterns of alafia, etawa, and ejife will always mean yes (bear in mind the nuances of "yes"); the patterns of oyekun and okana will always mean no.

1. The first question that should be asked is "Abeku si?" (Is something lacking?) It is possible that something was missed in the reading, and the diviner must consider this. If the answer to "Abeku si?" is yes, the diviner must consider, carefully and thoroughly, the client's question and the orisha's response. He may not have advised this person as well as he should have. If he is satisfied that he has missed nothing, it is ebó that is missing and the diviner must prescribe something that will help close the pattern.

2. The second question that the diviner should ask is, "Ebó elese [orisha's name]?" Although okana and oyekun may bring up issues with egun, the first consideration is always the orisha to whom Obí was cast. This spirit has the first option to claim something from the client. If the answer to this is yes, appropriate ebó or eboses must be marked. Note that if the diviner has used the system of aperes in conjunction with Elegguá, both Elegguá and the orisha who spoke through apere must be offered ebó. This may be broken into a series of questions to ensure that there is no mistake in the process of divination:

   ✠ "Ebó elese Elegguá?" If yes, the orisha is satisfied, and ebó must be marked. If the answer to this is no, the next question must be asked.

   ✠ "Ebó elese [name of orisha who spoke in apere]?" If the answer to this question is yes, the orisha is satisfied and ebó must be marked. If the answer is no, the next question must be asked.

   ✠ "Ebó elese Elegguá y [name of orisha who spoke in the apere]?" If the answer to this question is yes, the orishas should be offered ebó together; something must now be marked. If the answer to all these questions is no, the diviner must continue asking questions from this list.

3. The next question that the diviner should ask is "Ebó elese egun?" Although oyekun is the signature that enforces the needs of the dead, egun may also come through okana to claim offerings and worship; when trying to close a session with Obi, the diviner should consider this. Egun must always be given the opportunity to speak. If the answer to this question is no, the diviner continues with items from this list.

4. If neither the orisha to whom Obí was given nor egun will take ebó, the diviner must now ask, "Larishe si?" to see if

there is any remedy to the osogbos brought by this reading. If the answer to "Larishe si?" is yes, he must continue this line of questioning by marking ebó. Before pursuing the type of ebó to be made, however, he marks to which orisha the *larishe* (remedy) is directed. He does this by asking a series of questions:

❦ First, the diviner asks, "Elese Elegguá?" for he is the orisha who comes before all others. He can prescribe larishe for all situations.

❦ Second, the diviner should ask, "Elese Egun?" for egun may always speak through both okana and oyekun. Just as Elegguá can prescribe a larishe for all situations, so can one's own egun do the same.

❦ Third, if an apere was read before Elegguá, the orisha who spoke in that apere must be questioned. The diviner asks, "Elese [orisha's name]?" If this is the spirit offering a larishe to the sign, part of this larishe must go to Elegguá, as the two spirits spoke together. They will also work together to benefit the supplicant.

❦ Finally, the diviner must ask this question for the orishas who speak in the final sign that appeared for this reading, either okana or oyekun. For each spirit, he asks, "Elese [orisha's name]?" If none of these takes larishe, we say that the larishe lies with the client's own head. It must be given a rogación; if that does not close the oracle, *eborí* (feeding of the head) should be prescribed as well. All this must be done at either the feet of this person's crowning orisha or at the feet of Obatalá if that orisha is not known.

If these things are not enough to close the oracle, the diviner must continue to search for something that will.

Note: If "Larishe si?" answers yes, this changes the implications of Obí's final pattern. Obviously, because one is asking this series of questions, the oracle did not close out on a positive note; the orisha questioned did not promise full attainment. By marking a larishe, the orisha is telling the diviner that more might be gained from the client's pursuit. This is a remedy for the osogbo predicted, and this must be kept in mind. It does not promise full success; it promises only greater blessings and a more satisfying outcome.

5. If that was fruitless, and if there are other priests and priestesses in the room, the diviner should ask, "Igboro larishe?" This question asks if an initiate in the room has the remedy to the client's situation. If yes, those in attendance are asked to speak, and after their pronouncements and prescriptions are made, Obí must again be asked for closure. This should be continued until either Obí closes or all have had the chance to speak. If all the priests and priestesses in the room have offered their advice and the oracle still will not close, the diviner must start again at the beginning of this list.

6. Having come this far into the session without closure, the diviner must now consider the patterns that came in relation to the client's question. Those spirits who speak in either okana or oyekun must be given a chance to close the session. One by one, the diviner should ask, "[orisha's name] onire?" which means "Will [orisha's name] give a blessing to close this sign?" When one is found who will give a blessing to the client, the oracle is closed; the diviner, however, should mark several eboses to this spirit using his own aché so that the blessing stays and is not lost.

7. If the diviner has come this far and all of Obí's letters are still negative, he is heated and must be removed from the house. The black rinds that are showing are oiled, watered, and cast into the street. Immediately a new coconut must be opened, and the diviner must pray again before

the orisha to whom Obí was cast. He relates what happened during the session and asks the spirit if all is well. If yes, the session is closed; Obí took the heat of the reading and the client is clear. He should be given several cleansing eboses, however, to ensure that nothing remains with him. If the letter has not been cleared (you know this when Obí gives another negative response), the diviner must try again to mark something that will close the session and bring a blessing. Further refusals to close mark serious spiritual issues that must be addressed by the diloggún.

Marking Ebó with Obí

Having determined that another ebó is needed before the session can be closed, the following questions must be asked, in their proper sequence. Along with these questions I indicate what the diviner must do if the answer is yes. (See pages 129–150 for specific eboses.)

Adimú? An adimú is an offering, often something edible although this is not a requirement. If the orisha marks adimú as the condition lacking, the diviner should then prescribe something based on his knowledge of what the orisha likes, taking into consideration the severity of the client's spiritual condition. Once he has made his prescription, the oracle should again be asked for closure.

Eboshure? A yes response means the spirit is requesting an ebó made of anything that can be eaten. The diviner should tell the client what foods the orisha likes and have him provide something for that spirit. The food left in *eboshure* remains with the orisha until it begins to spoil. Once the diviner has made his prescription, the oracle should again be asked for closure.

Ebó keun edun keun? A yes means a daily cleansing must be done before the orisha's shrine. Each day something different is used. The diviner must use his own aché to determine what fruits, grains, or other items are to be used in the cleansings. Once these prescriptions have been given, the oracle should be asked for closure.

Ebó misi? A yes marks a spiritual bath that must be taken by the client. Using his own aché, the diviner marks the items to be used and the number of times the bath is to be taken. The oracle must be asked for closure.

Egun onire? A yes marks that egun will remove the volatile heat of this letter. The diviner must determine if they want anything in return for their help (the question to be asked now is "Ebó elese egun?"). If no ebó is required, we say that these spirits love the client for free, but a token adimú should still be given. It is through their propitiation that the oracle will find closure. Before assuming closure, however, the diviner must still ask, "Eboda?"

Igboro Larishe? A yes means the remedy will come from the priests or priestesses present at the mat. They should be allowed to give the client eboses and advice. Any ebó prescribed by any priest or priestess in the room should be done as if the orishas prescribed it themselves. These will be the works that clear the osogbo in the sign that fell. The diviner may then ask the oracle for closure.

Ebó kere? *Ebó kere* is a beautiful, yet complicated set of offerings. It consists of several spiritual cleansings for the client. A yees means that using his own aché, the diviner must prescribe the following things: the series of offerings to be used for the cleansings, the length of time that this is to be done, and what is to be done with each offering when it is replaced with the next. For example, consider that Yemayá has stood up for ebó, and Obí declares that she wants ebó kere. Because her number is seven, he decides that each offering should remain with her for seven days, and he marks the following items for a period of four weeks (one month): a watermelon, molasses, flowers, and a basket of fruit. After describing the offerings, he decides where each offering should be taken after one is removed and the next given. In this example, the diviner decides that each should be taken to a lake for disposal, so as the offerings are removed and replenished, the client takes the old ones to a lake. This completes the ebó of ebó kere, and Obí may be asked for closure.

Sarayeye? A yes marks that a cleansing is needed. Using the diviner's own aché, the item with which the client should be cleansed is marked. Sometimes, this can be an animal. In *sarayeye,* however, it is customary for the animal to be set free after the cleansing, as no sacrifice was dictated by the oracle (if a blood sacrifice is needed for a cleansing, the odu will dictate that *eyebale,* "sacrifice," is needed). Finally, the method of disposal should be marked as well (if the cleansing is done with an animal, the oracle should dictate where the animal is to be set free). After these things have been explained to the client, the oracle may be asked for closure.

Koborí eledá? A yes prescribes an ebó made to one's orí. Usually, this is a rogación (a cleansing of the head), but the diviner should mark the things that need to be used in the rogación. Depending on the problems faced by the client and the pattern that has fallen, the rogación might need to be done at the feet of a specific orisha. The oracle will dictate when this is the case. This type of offering will not dictate the "feeding" of the orí with sacrifice; such an ebó would be marked by eyebale (animal sacrifice). Having determined these things, the oracle may be asked for closure.

Kaure? A yes asks for prayers made to either egun or an orisha. The prayers should be dictated to the client. In *kaure,* it is customary for the client to make adimú with a candle before the prayer and with fruit once the prayers are completed. When all this information has been described, the oracle may be asked for closure.

If the oracle will take none of these, we say the larishe is eyebale, or the sacrifice of an animal. Blood offerings are very hot and volatile; it is important to note that this is always a last resort for ebó. Life on all levels is a precious gift, and it is taken, reverently, only when there are no other options. Having determined that eyebale is the ebó needed by the orisha, the diviner must ask Obí for closure with the question, "Eboda?" If it will not close, this entire process is begun again.

Eboses for the Orishas

When prescribing ebó based the oracle Obí, the diviner is limited only by his imagination and those things that he knows the orishas like. This list, therefore, is not exhaustive; it consists of examples of the types of offerings that can be made to each spirit.

Ebó Elese Elegguá (Ebó at the Feet of Elegguá)

❧ To obtain blessings from Elegguá, the following ebó should be prepared. Three fresh fish should be baked, oiled liberally with epó while cooking. A dish of yellow rice should be prepared, and it should be placed on a white serving platter. The three baked fish are put on the bed of rice and all is served to Elegguá overnight. The following morning, the ebó is wrapped in brown paper and taken to a crossroads with a derecho of twenty-one pennies.

❧ If Obí has marked a cleansing before Elegguá, this ebó will help remove negative energies from the client. Three fresh eggs must be purchased from the market, and these are brought to Elegguá with a container of epó, a bottle of rum, and a cigar. Before Elegguá's shrine, the client must pray for release from osogbo, greasing the eggs with the red palm oil while he prays. Once he is done, he sprays each egg with a mouthful of rum and a mouthful of cigar smoke and puts each into a single brown paper bag. Standing tall before Eshu, the supplicant rubs the bag over his entire body, making sure that the paper touches every part. He should repeat this several times, and with each pass he must pray that Eshu takes the osogbo predicted by Obí. This bag is left with Elegguá overnight, and the following morning it is taken to the crossroad with a derecho of twenty-one cents.

If the osogbo given by Obí was severe, the client will need to visit three crossroads the next morning, dropping twenty-one pennies and breaking one egg from the bag at each junction. Once the last egg is broken, the client cleanses himself with the empty bag one last time and that is left at the crossroads as well. He must return home by a separate route.

- If the osogbo predicted by Obí is severe, this ebó will lift some of those negative energies. Into three small brown paper bags the following ingredients should be placed: three pennies, smoked fish, jutía, and toasted corn. Epó should be poured lightly over these, and the bags are sealed. Using one bag at a time, the client must cleanse himself with these before Elegguá. They are left with him overnight; the following morning, they are taken to a crossroads.

- If economic concerns have brought this person before the orishas, the following ebó to Elegguá will help settle his finances. The client should return to the diviner's house with the following items: uncooked cornmeal, smoked fish, jutía, epó, honey, a white plate, and four pennies. In front of Elegguá, the client should pray for the prosperity that he needs, and while he prays he should mix together the cornmeal, smoked fish, and jutía in a large bowl. A generous amount of epó should be poured into this, followed by an equally generous amount of honey. With his hands, these things should be formed into a thick paste, from which four balls must be formed. Placing the cornmeal balls on the white plate, he should insert one penny into each ball, again praying for the abundance needed. These are left with Eshu overnight, and the following morning one ball must be placed outside at each corner of the house or apartment in which the client lives. Returning to Elegguá, the supplicant must explain that adimú has been placed all around the house so that all within can enjoy Elegguá's blessings of prosperity.

Ebó Elese Ogún (Ebó at the Feet of Ogún)

✲ If Ogún has brought osogbo to the client through Obí, the client needs to be cleansed. The following ebó can be done to remove the negativity. A pound of ground beef is put into a large mixing bowl, and to this is added a liberal amount of epó and rum. These things are mixed thoroughly and then divided into seven equal parts. Each part must be put into a brown paper bag. With one bag, the client rubs himself from head to toe before Ogún, praying that he protect him from all harm.

The ebó should then be taken to the railroad tracks, and there the bag that was used to clean the body is thrown onto the middle of the tracks. Once done, each of the remaining six bags is used to rub the following parts of the car that took the client to the railroad: each tire, the front fender, and the back fender. As a bag is used, it is thrown to Ogún at the railroad tracks. The client should pray the entire time that the orisha save him and his riders from accidents.

If ebó needs to be made before Elegguá and Ogún, this may be adapted for the two of them. Divide the ground meat into eight parts—one is used to cleanse the client before Eshu first, and then another is used to cleanse him to Ogún. When the ebó is done in this manner, the client must first visit a crossroads where the bag used for Elegguá is left; include a derecho of twenty-one pennies. The remainder of the ebó is still done at the railroad tracks, and the car is to be cleansed there.

❡ If Obí has marked danger to the client's home through a session with Ogún, this ebó will save him from disaster. Behind the front door, Ogún is fed a young rooster. Some of this blood must be smeared on the door's frame, along with some of the honey from the sacrifice. When Ogún is cleansed, the door is cleansed as well. Seven days later, when Ogún is given a basket of cool fruits, the door's frame is smeared with cocoa butter. Osogbo will not visit this person's house if these things are done.

❡ If Ogún requires an adimú through Obí, the following items should be put in a large gourd: toasted corn, seven pennies, smoked fish, jutía, honey, grated coconut, and epó. The gourd is presented to Ogún with two green seven-day candles. Once the flames have consumed the candles, the gourd and its contents are left beside railroad tracks in the woods.

❡ When the client is trying to claim blessings at Okun's feet, the following ebó will help. A large ñame is purchased in Ogún's name, and this is brought before the orisha's cauldron. The client's name is written on brown paper, and a slit is cut into the top of the ñame; the opening is made just large enough to hold the piece of brown paper. The entire root is slathered with epó, and it is used to cleanse the client from head to toe. Set on Ogún's cauldron, this ebó is left with him indefinitely until it rots; when this happens, it is taken to a lonely section of railroad tracks in the woods. If a vine grows from this ebó while it sits with Ogún, this signifies good fortune.

Ebó elese Ochosi (Ebó at the Feet of Ochosi)

There are times when Ochosi stands up in a reading to warn a client that an enemy will soon do him harm. If the name of this enemy can be determined, or if the name is already known, this ebó will render his or her efforts harmless. On a brown piece of paper, the client must write the enemy's name using a lead pencil, not ink. The back and front of the paper are then smeared with epó, and the paper is folded three times before being impaled on Ochosi's arrow. Blowing rum and cigar smoke over the orishas, the client should pray to him that the named enemy is rendered harmless by the forces of justice. To finish this ebó, two white candles are lit to Ochosi in the name of justice. He will protect the client from this enemy.

If Ochosi has stood up through Obí for an adimú, the following dish will appease him. For this ebó, the client will need two pounds of hard corn (the type used for chicken feed), a fresh coconut, three tablespoons of epó, one large white onion. Soak the corn overnight so that it becomes soft. The next morning, crack open a fresh coconut and remove the black skin from the meat; grate this finely over a terra-cotta plate until a bed of coconut is formed. Set this aside.

In a large iron skillet, melt the epó over medium heat. Grate the onion finely into this. Sauté until the onion begins to turn translucent. Once the onion is thoroughly sautéed, add the corn on top of this. Stir the onion and corn continually so that they do not burn; continue to sauté the ingredients until they are thoroughly cooked. Remove them from the heat, spooning the corn and onion over the bed of coconut. This is served to Ochosi and left with him overnight.

Ebó elese Babaluaiye (Ebó at the Feet of Babaluaiye)

✘ If Obi marked that a cleansing needs to be done before
Asohano's shrine, the following bath will remove the
osogbo that stands in the way of the client's evolution.

Purchase the herbs romerillo, cundiamor, and bledo blanco
(available from a botánica). To complete this ritual you will also
need seven ears of roasted corn, sackcloth, honey, epó, dry white
wine, a paper bag, a cigar, and seventeen pennies.

Shred the herbs into a large vat and soak overnight in fresh
water. The next day, wring out the herbs well, until the liquid turns
a dark green. Strain this herbal water and discard the plant material. Pour the herbal water into seven jars.

Nightly for seven nights, the client must bathe with the liquid
from one jar. While bathing, he should scrub himself with one of
the ears of corn. Once the bath is done, this corn is placed on the
sackcloth before Babaluaiye. After the seventh bath, all seven ears
of corn should be smeared with the honey and epó. Spray the
wine over them and place all in the paper bag, then seal with smoke
from the cigar. The next morning, leave everything by the gate of
a cemetery with seventeen cents as Babaluaiye's derecho.

✘ When financial concerns have brought the client to the
oracle, if Babaluaiye stands up for ebó, the following
adimú might help solve these problems. Two white seven-
day candles, seven fresh bread rolls, seven ears of corn
roasted in epó, a white plate, and sackcloth should be
brought to the orisha. Before presenting the ebó, the
candles are lit and the client must pray, silently, for the
abundance that is needed.

When he has finished his prayers, the food is set on the white
plate, and this is set on top of the sackcloth. As long as the candles
burn, the adimú is left with Babaluaiye. When the candles burn
out, the food is wrapped in the sackcloth with a derecho of seventeen cents. All must be left under a bush in the woods so that the
earth can consume the offering.

✹ If there have been one or more people in the client's house suffering from disease, or if a family member is chronically ill, an osogbo marked through Babaluaiye could indicate the need to cleanse the house of illness. To begin this ebó, it is important that the client scrub his dwelling thoroughly, leaving no trace of dirt anywhere in the house. As fresh air and sunshine are important to the physical and spiritual disinfecting process, open wide all the doors and windows.

Once this is done, fill a large basin with fresh water and soak cundiamor (an herb sacred to this orisha) in that water. Place this under the sickbed first. Every day, this bowl should be moved to another room until it sits by the front door. There, seventeen pennies are added to the water, and it is thrown out the next day in the woods. Pray to Asohano that he remove the sickness with the water.

Note: If Obí marks ebó to be done to both Babaluaiye and Elegguá, the ebó must be given to Afrá, which is the Eshu received when Babaluaiye is washed for an initiate. It may not go to the Elegguá that stood at the priest's feet for ocha, nor may it be given to the client's Elegguá if he has received the initiation of the warriors. Only Afrá may work with Asohano.

Ebó elese Aganyú (Ebó at the feet of Aganyú)

✹ If the client is recovering from extensive illness and Aganyú has stood up through Obí, a cleansing might serve to satisfy osogbo and close the session. For this bath, the client must bring the following things to the diviner's home: a large white basin, twelve pieces of okra that have been diced very fine, a bar of pure Castile soap (cocoa butter soap may also be used), a complete change of white clothes, two white seven-day candles, and a large white plate. The diviner pours very warm water into the white basin, and the okra is soaked in this, then whipped briskly until it thickens. During this, the priest must pray to Aganyú that he remove the osogbo from the person for whom the bath is prepared.

Once this is done, the client draws a warm bath and washes himself with the soap that was brought for the ebó; he dips this soap into the thickened okra mixture and then scrubs himself thoroughly. No part of the body must remain unwashed. Once he is clean, the rest of the bath is poured from the shoulders down, and he soaks in this until the diviner comes to dry him and dress him in a change of white clothes. The supplicant is then led before Aganyú's shrine, where he lights the two white candles, setting them on the white plate. He then prays for the return of his health and the removal of sickness.

If the osogbo faced is severe, or if Obí will not give closure from this ebó, other elements might be added. The diviner should question Aganyú about a rogación before his shrine, and the bath might need to be repeated for nine nights. These options must be investigated before considering the ebó complete.

❧ Special petitions may be made of Aganyú by forming a tower for him. To complete this ebó, the client will need the following items: a pound of cornmeal, okra (with the seeds removed), honey, jutía, smoked fish, epó, a red cloth, and a red candle. The cornmeal and okra are cooked together over low heat in a small amount of water. Stir constantly so it does not burn, until it forms a thick paste. More water may be added while the ingredients cook if needed. Once a thick paste is formed, the cornmeal and okra are removed from the heat. Stir in the honey, jutía, fish, and epó. Form a tall tower when the mixture cools, and cover with the red cloth. The client presents this adimú to Aganyú, lighting a red candle and praying for his request. When the candle is consumed, the tower is taken to the woods and left beside a tall tree.

❦ Aganyú is an orisha that likes large offerings of fruits. To obtain his favor, on a mat of red cloth the client should bring him plantains smeared with honey and epó, bananas, pineapples, apples, and plates of unsalted crackers smeared with epó. All should be left with him until the fruits begin to turn; they are then removed and taken to the foot of a large tree.

Note: Because Aganyú and Shangó are father and son, any ebó that can be given to one may also be given to the other—they both adore the same things.

Ebó elese Shangó (Ebó at the Feet of Shangó)

❦ Shangó is an orisha who likes to eat, and when Obí has marked that an adimú is wanted by him, the diviner should consider prescribing some of his favorite cooked dishes. One of his favorites is *amalá.* To prepare this dish, the supplicant must bring the following ingredients to the diviner's home: two pounds of yellow cornmeal, salt, and 3/4 cup of epó. The one preparing ebó should salute Shangó, telling him that he is preparing his favorite dish. He should mention his spiritual needs at this time, as well. Immediately, he should begin his preparations, for Shangó will be hungry!

Put the cornmeal and a dash of salt into a large pan with eight cups of water. Stir continually over medium-high heat until it boils. The moment it begins to boil, turn the heat to low and continue stirring until the mixture is very thick. Remove from the stove, stir the epó in immediately, put into a large serving dish, and give to Shangó. Note that if one is trying to sweeten Shangó to one's desires, brown sugar and honey may be mixed into the amalá before it is served; as is sweetened, so is Shangó sweetened to the client.

❦ Shangó is fond of bananas, almost as much as he likes amalá. The two foods can be combined into a sweet delicacy for the orisha, and with this dish Shangó can be persuaded to help lift almost any osogbo that he has marked. In addition to the ingredients needed for the sweet amalá given above, the client will need six bananas, a liberal amount of toasted cornmeal, a roll of wax paper, additional epó, and a rolling pin. The sweet amalá is prepared and allowed to cool completely. The bananas are peeled, and the toasted cornmeal is sprinkled on a flat dish. Once the sweet amalá has cooled, six flat portions of it are rolled between pieces of wax paper. Set the bananas on these sheets of amalá and roll into them tight bundles. Melted epó is brushed over these rolled bananas, and they are then coated with the toasted cornmeal. Serve this to Shangó while lighting two red candles and praying for the evolution desired.

❡ Finally, there is a cold dish that can be made and served to Shangó. It requires a minimum of cooking but is still favored by the orisha. To make this dish, known as *obeguede,* a pound of okra must be finely diced and put into a mixing bowl with two pounds of cornmeal. Add just a bit of water and stir. Continue to add water a little bit at a time, stirring well until a thick paste is formed. Six balls should be made from this, and they are served to Shangó on a red platter. If the client wants to sweeten the orisha to his desires, he may drizzle honey over the obeguede while praying to Shangó.

Again, note that any ebó made to Shangó may also be made to Aganyú. Because they are father and son, they both adore the same offerings.

Ebó Elese Obatalá (Ebó at the Feet of Obatalá)

❡ If Obí has marked a spiritual bath at the feet of Obatalá as the solution to the client's osogbo, herbal waters will cure this person's afflictions. The client must return to the priest's house with the following herbs (available from a botánica) for this bath: albahaca, altamisa, colonia, maravilla, malva, chicoria, altea, and white lilies. In addition, he should bring Florida water, holy water, coconut milk, an egg, and eight jars. The diviner will boil the herbs in a large basin of water until the essences are extracted. The infusion is allowed to cool, and the herbs are then strained and wrung out of the bath. The herbal wastes should be returned to the earth. To the cooled infusion, add liberal amounts of the Florida water, holy water, and coconut milk. Only the white of the egg is added to this; the egg yolk is discarded. Once everything is mixed well, it is poured into the eight jars and the client may take home the bath.

Once a night for eight nights, the client must take one bath with the herbal infusion. The water is poured from the shoulders down (never touching the head as it is poured). He then washes himself thoroughly, praying to Obatalá that his body be cooled as the osogbo is removed. Each night after the bath, he is to sleep dressed in white, and he must spend his day dressed in white as well.

♛ To appease Obatalá before asking him to intercede with difficulties, do the following. Nine small fish should be fried in sunflower oil. Do not season them with salt—cook them plain. While the fish are frying, prepare a pan of white rice without salt. On a small plate, one of these fish should be put on a bed of white rice—that portion goes to Elegguá. The rest of the rice goes onto a large white serving platter with the fish on top. This large portion goes on top of Obatalá's sopera with two unlit white candles. The ebó must sit with the orishas for four days. At the end of this time, the two portions are wrapped separately in brown paper. Elegguá's should be taken to the crossroads with a derecho of three cents, and Obatalá's goes to either a small hill or a ceiba tree with a derecho of eight cents. Once these adimús have been removed, the two white candles are lit to Obatalá and the client may pray for his special request.

- Another ebó that may be done to appease the orisha consists of boiled ñame, white rice, cocoa butter, coconut milk, cascarilla, and eight pennies. First, the ñame must be peeled and boiled until it is soft. In a large mixing bowl, mash it thoroughly. The white rice, cocoa butter, coconut milk, and cascarilla are added to this, and everything is mashed together until a paste forms.

A large white serving platter should be covered with white cotton and sprinkled liberally with cascarilla. Once this is done, divide the ñame mixture into eight equal portions and form into eight separate balls. Roll each ball in cascarilla before putting it on top of the cotton. Insert one penny into each ball. Sprinkle the entire ebó once more with cascarilla and cover it with more white cotton. The balls are then put on top of Obatalá's sopera with two unlit, white, seven-day candles.

For four days this ebó is left with him; at the end of this time, use Obí to determine where the ñame balls are to be discarded. They must be taken to that place immediately, wrapped in brown paper. Returning home, the client may light the white candles and pray about his needs. As long as the candles burn, the client should spend some time each day praying to Obatalá.

- Finally, if the client aspires only to personal evolution (whether it is spiritual, financial, emotional, or physical), he should make a tall white tower from cooked, unsalted white rice and cocoa butter. It is served to Obatalá by placing it on a white plate, covering the entire ebó with a fine sprinkling of cascarilla. A white seven-day candle should be lit; once burned out, the orisha must be asked with Obí where he wants his ebó deposited. To ensure that he always evolves, the client should then place a fresh ñame (the whole root, uncooked and unpeeled) coated with cascarilla on that white plate. A vine will grow from the root; when it begins to grow, the client's personal evolution will unfold. This root may eventually spoil, having absorbed the negativity holding back this person from his goals. With Obí, Obatalá should be asked where the ñame is to be discarded, and then a new one should be given to him.

Ebó Elese Oyá (Ebó at the Feet of Oyá)

❦ Like her lover, Shangó, Oyá is an orisha who adores food and loves to eat. When Obí marks that an ebó is needed for Oyá, the following food will satisfy her tastes. It is known as *aguidí* (this is also favored by Aganyú, and may be made for him as well). The client should return to the diviner's house with the following ingredients: two pounds of yellow cornmeal, three cups of water, three tablespoons of vinegar, one sour orange, one cup of milk, one and a half cups of brown sugar, two cups of raisins, three teaspoons of vanilla extract, a cinnamon stick and the juice of one lemon. Put the cornmeal into a large mixing bowl; into this add the water, the vinegar, and the juice of one sour orange. Stir well, then let this sit uncovered for two days so that the mixture can ferment.

At the end of the second day, the liquid is strained out and three fresh cups of water are added. Set the pan on the stove over low heat. Stir constantly until all the liquid evaporates. Add the final ingredients to this: the milk, the brown sugar, the raisins, the vanilla extract, a cinnamon stick, and the juice of one lemon. Continue to cook over low heat until all the liquids evaporate and only a thick paste remains. Cool, form into nine balls, and serve to Oyá on a platter.

- Another cooked dish that may be served to Oyá is called olelé. To prepare this meal for her, the client must return to the diviner's home with the following ingredients: a pound of black-eyed peas, two eggs, saffron, a medium onion, a red bell pepper, and six cloves of garlic, epó, $^1/_2$ cup tomato sauce, black pepper, and a roll of aluminum foil. Soak the black-eyed peas overnight, and the next morning rub them to remove all the peels. In a large bowl, mash these until they form a thick paste; water may be added during this process if needed. Into the mashed peas add the eggs and a small pinch of saffron. Set this mixture aside.

Next, dice the onion, bell pepper, and garlic. In a saucepan over medium heat, melt three tablespoons of epó and add the onion mixture. When the onion has become translucent, add the tomato sauce and $^1/_2$ teaspoon of black pepper. Stir this for four minutes, until the sauce becomes a shiny red. Once that color is brought out, add the bean mixture and mix well. Remove from the heat.

From the aluminum foil, cut nine large squares and divide the thickened mixture evenly among them. Wrap them tightly like a tamale and boil in a large pan for half an hour. Drain and cool. Unwrap them once they are cooled, and serve to Oyá on a large white serving platter.

- If Obí has marked a cleansing to Oyá as ebó, the following will remove the energies bringing osogbo to the client. For this offering, these items should be brought to the diviner's house: an eggplant, a white plate, nine hard candies, nine slices of fresh coconut, nine white votive candles, a brown paper bag. The eggplant is cut into nine equal pieces; they are then set on the white plate. The hard candies, the pieces of coconut, and the votive candles are put on the plate as well.

The supplicant should pay foribale to Oyá once the ebó is prepared, praying for a release from osogbo. One by one, each item on the plate is rubbed over the body thoroughly. The candles are lit on the plate after the client cleans himself with them. Each item except the candles is placed in the paper bag. The bag must be sealed, and all these things remain with Oyá overnight. The next morning, they are taken to the gates of a cemetery with a derecho of nine pennies.

Ebó Elese Oshún (Ebó at the Feet of Oshún)

☙ When Obí marks an adimú to Oshún, she should be spoiled with her favorite foods. Among these is a dish called *natilla.* To prepare this cooked food, the client should bring the following ingredients to the diviner's house: a can of evaporated milk, some white sugar, a cinnamon stick, salt, cornstarch, an egg, and some vanilla extract. In a large microwavable bowl, stir together $^3/_4$ cup of evaporated milk and $^1/_4$ cup of water. Remove $^1/_4$ cup of the mixture and set aside in a small bowl. In the large bowl of water and milk, combine the following ingredients: $1^1/_2$ tablespoons of sugar, the cinnamon stick, and a pinch of salt. Microwave this on high for one minute and twenty-five seconds.

While this is heating, in the smaller bowl of milk and water combine: $1^1/_2$ tablespoons of cornstarch and the yolk of one egg. Whip well. Once the mixture in the microwave is done, stir the cornstarch mixture into the heated liquid, stirring continually until the ingredients thicken. Reset the microwave to medium-high heat and cook for an additional two minutes (it may take a bit longer), until the mixture is thick. Remove. Add 1/4 teaspoon of vanilla extract and stir, then serve to Oshún in an attractive bowl.

☙ Baked oranges are another delicacy favored by Oshún. For this ebó, the client should return to the diviner's house with the following ingredients: two pounds of yams, five large sweet oranges, butter, sugar, orange juice, four eggs, and salt. Begin by preheating the oven to 375 degrees.

Wash and peel the yams, cut them into small pieces, and bring them to a boil. Let boil until they are soft.

While the yams are cooking, cut out the tops of the oranges, making sure that the hole is large enough to remove the pulp without destroying the shell (if the shell is destroyed, Oshún will not take the ebó). The pulp is discarded. Once the yams are soft, drained off the water and mash with butter, sugar, orange juice, egg yolks (do not use the whites but save them for meringue below), and salt. Mash until all the ingredients are mixed well. Divide the mixture into five equal parts and fill the empty orange shells with this. The stuffed shells are then put on a baking sheet and cooked for fifteen minutes. When they are done, remove, cool, and serve to Oshún on a pretty yellow platter.

If the supplicant wishes to sweeten Oshún to his desires, add honey and a meringue to the top of the oranges once they are cooked and cooled. To prepare this meringue add yellow food coloring to the saved egg whites. With a mixer at high speed, beat them until they begin to foam. Once this foam forms, add one tablespoon of sugar at a time for a total of four, continuing to beat until the whites are stiff, white, and shiny. Let the oranges cool, glaze them with honey, and spoon the meringue over the top of the open shell.

⚜ If Obí has determined that the client must take a bath in honor of Oshún to remove osogbo, the following might help. The client should return to the client's house with the herbs myrtle, vervain, lettuce, lavender, and watercress. He must also bring claret, honey, cinnamon, five egg yolks, two yellow candles, and a complete change of white clothes. The diviner must boil the herbs in a large pot until the water is dark; the herbal wastes are then strained and wrung out of the liquid. To the liquid add the wine, honey, cinnamon, and egg yolks. The client is washed from the shoulders down, and is then allowed to bathe freely. After a quick shower to remove the residue, he is dried, dressed, in white, and taken to Oshún. He salutes her, then lights the two yellow candles and prays that his cleansing is made complete. If the osogbo of this sign is severe, this bath should be repeated nightly for five nights.

Ebó Elese Yemayá (Ebó at the Feet of Yemayá)

☙ When an osogbo comes from Yemayá, a cleansing to her will help lift this negativity. For this ebó, the client must find his oldest clothes; he is to dress in these for the ebó. He must also have a jar of molasses, seven pennies, and a complete change of new white clothes. Dressing in the old clothing, he goes to the beach and stands before Yemayá; the molasses is in one hand, the seven pennies in the other. Entering the sea by walking sideways, he goes out in the ocean until he is waist-deep (no farther) and pours a tight circle of sweet molasses around himself.

Once this circle is there, he stands facing the horizon and prays to Yemayá to release him from those things that hold him back in life. He must then wait until Yemayá covers him in a wave; once the wave washes over his head, he releases the pennies into the water and strips off his clothes. Naked and cleansed, he goes back to the shore and dresses in white from head to toe. *Note:* It is important for the client not to lose the empty molasses jar in the ocean. To do so would be an offense to the orisha.

☙ When the client has seven prayers that must be answered, the following ebó will help him attain his desires. For this offering, he will need a large sheet of brown paper, a watermelon, seven pennies, molasses, blue cloth, a blue platter, and two blue seven-day candles. The brown paper is cut into seven pieces, and on each piece the client must write a separate wish. Seven holes are cut into the watermelon (keept the rinds), and one wish is stuffed into each hole. Over each paper is placed one penny, and molasses is poured into each hole. The rinds are then put back into the watermelon to seal it and the whole ebó is wrapped in blue cloth. All this goes on the blue platter before Yemayá, and on either side a blue seven-day candle is lit to her while the supplicant prays for his desires. When the candles are consumed, the melon is thrown into the ocean.

✹ If Yemayá has demanded adimú through Obí, the following dish should satisfy her tastes. It is called *ekru-aro,* and although it has only two ingredients, it is a bit complicated to prepare. For this, the client will need to procure a pound of black-eyed peas, two eggs, a roll of aluminum foil, and some cotton twine. The beans should be washed and soaked overnight; the next day, they are rubbed well until all the peels are removed. With just a few dashes of water, mash them until a thick paste forms. Be very stingy when adding water; more can always be added later, but if too much is added, the paste is ruined. Once a thick paste is created, add the eggs and continue to mash and mix well. Seven squares of aluminum foil should be cut, and the mixture is evenly divided among these. These squares are folded tightly like tamales, and are then tied with the twine so they will not open. In a large pan of boiling water, cook these for thirty minutes. Then remove, allow to cool, and unwrap. The ekru-aro should be placed before to Yemayá on a blue serving dish.

Note: One may also prepare a bed of white or yellow rice while the ekru-aro is boiling; do not add salt to the rice. This goes on the serving platter first and the ekru rests on top of this. It may also be garnished with fresh herbs to make the sacrifice more visually appealing.

Ebó Elese Egun (Ebó at the Feet of Egun)

When making ebó to egun, it seems they prefer food over any other type of offering; this makes sense, as one's egun were once alive and loved to eat. My favorite ebó to them is not traditional. It is a recipe that was sent out through a newsgroup in which I participate, and using Obí itself I found that it was something they adore. This recipe uses okra, an ingredient that has an interesting story behind it.

Okra, so the legend goes, is not native to American shores; it was brought over by slaves as they were forced to endure the Middle Passage. The seeds were smuggled on the ships by a small group of African women—they were hidden in their hair, and if the traders saw them, they thought it was only "dirt" embedded in their curls. Once these women were in the New World, they planted the seeds of the okra to remind them of their native lands, and okra soon became an important element in many eboses to the orishas, especially Shangó, Aganyú, and egun. It also became a staple food in the Americas; whenever ones eats okra or uses it in a recipe, it is available only because of these ancestors.

The recipe that I received is called Fried Okra and Potatoes; it is one that I have adapted, as it used salt, which is anathema to egun, and olive oil, which is not traditional to African-based religion. To the original recipe I have also added yellow rice; the original dish was oily, and rice absorbs this oil. Epó (the oil that I use in place of olive oil) is a powerful ingredient in ebó for egun, and if it is saved in the dish and not drained away, it gives more aché to the offering. Rice is also a grain loved by egun, and it adds to the ebó's appeal. My version of the recipe appears here.

To prepare this dish, you will need yellow rice, one pound of fresh okra, two large baking potatoes, one medium white onion, $^1/_2$ cup of cornmeal, $^1/_4$ teaspoon of ground black pepper, and $^1/_2$ cup of epó. Cook the yellow rice according to the package's directions; however, do not use salt in its preparation. While the rice is cooking, cut the stems from the okra. Wash it and cut into half-inch pieces. Because there is a legend behind the okra seeds, these should be removed and put into a small dish, left on the *bóveda* (egun's shrine) in the kitchen to commemorate the ancestors who brought this religion, and the plant, from Africa. The potatoes should be washed, peeled, and diced into half-inch squares. The onion is also washed, peeled, and then finely grated. Once all these preparations are finished, put the potatoes, okra, and onion into a mixing bowl. Sprinkle the cornmeal and pepper over this and toss well.

In a large cast-iron skillet, melt the epó over medium-high heat. It must not be allowed to smoke; if it does, reduce the heat just a bit. The mixture of potatoes, okra, and onion is spooned carefully into the oil so that it does not splatter. Fry, stirring frequently, until everything is browned (this will take ten to fifteen minutes depending on how hot the epó is). When the potato and onion mixture is cooked, remove this pan from the heat. Spoon the yellow rice into a large serving dish, and over this spoon the contents of the skillet. This should be served to egun and left overnight.

- *Oguidí* is a homemade candy adored by the spirits known as egun; it is also favored by Elegguá. Therefore, whenever I make this candy as an ebó to egun, I also prepare it for Elegguá: the two work together closely, and it is always wise to have Eshu's goodwill when propitiating the dead.

Soak an entire box of cornmeal in a large bowl of fresh, cool water for three days; this ensures that the cornmeal will begin to ferment. After three days, add a single cinnamon stick, a cup of brown sugar, and a dash of vanilla. Put the mixture in a medium saucepan over a low flame and allow it to cook, stirring constantly so that the mixture does not burn. The water must be all but evaporated from of this mixture. Once done, two equal-size tamales should be made of this mixture with aluminum foil (see directions for ekru-aro on page 146), and they are boiled in a large pan of water for fifteen minutes.

Two platters should be prepared. Give one platter with an opened tamale first to Elegguá and put the second before Egun. Cover the candy with honey and molasses at their respective shrines while praying for sweetness to come back into your life. These offerings sit with the spirits for three days, then each is wrapped with brown paper and taken to a cemetery.

♟ Another cooked adimú that is adored by both egun and Elegguá is *plantanos borrachos,* or "drunken plantains." You will need red palm oil, nine ripe bananas, one stick of cinnamon, $^1/_2$ cup star anise seeds, one cup of honey, $^1/_2$ cup of sugarcane syrup, and one cup of dry red wine. (*Note:* Salt is never used when cooking for the spirits.)

Preheat the oven to 350 degrees F. Lightly grease a baking dish with the red palm oil. Remove the plantains from their skins and place them, side by side, in the dish. In a separate bowl, crush the cinnamon stick and star anise seeds and mix in the honey, then pour the mixture evenly over the plantains.

In a mixing bowl, blend the sugarcane syrup and the wine, then pour evenly over the plantains. Cover the baking dish with the aluminum foil and bake for forty-five minutes. Now uncover the dish and bake another five to ten minutes, or until the juices have thickened. (Watch carefully: you do not want the plantains to burn.) Remove from the oven and allow the plantains to cool.

Elegguá should sit with egun for three days while the dish is served to both together. At the end of three days, wrap the food in brown paper and take it to a cemetery.

Note: This ebó can be prepared for Shangó and Aganyú as well; the two love any dish prepared with plantains.

♟ Another adimú that can be prepared for one's egun is called *arroz con leche,* or "rice with milk." To prepare this, the client must purchase the following ingredients: milk, uncooked rice, cinnamon sticks, one lemon, white sugar, and white vanilla extract. In a large pot, two cups of water, one cinnamon stick, and a bit of finely grated lemon peel should be brought to a rolling boil. Add to this $^1/_2$ cup of uncooked rice. Reduce heat to low once the rice has been added, and stir well until the boiling ceases. Cover the pot and allow the rice to simmer until it is tender.

In a small bowl, mix together $^1/_2$ teaspoon of white vanilla extract, seven tablespoons of sugar, and $1^1/_2$ cups of milk. Mix this well. When the rice is tender, add the milk mixture to the rice; turn the heat back up to high and stir vigorously until it begins to boil. Reduce the heat to low once more, continuing to stir the rice, uncovered, until it thickens. Do not allow the milk to scald or the rice to burn. It will take another fifteen minutes of stirring and cooking before the rice thickens; when it does, the dish is done. It should be served in a bowl to egun while still steaming hot.

Mail-Order Sources for Religious Supplies

UNLESS ONE LIVES IN A MAJOR CITY, such as New York, Houston, Miami, Orlando, Chicago, Detroit, or Los Angeles, finding supplies for the Lucumí faith can be difficult. This appendix was created to help alleviate this. All of the botánicas listed are legitimate, headed by real priests and priestesses of various Afro-Cuban and Afrocentric religions. By no means is this list exhaustive; it only provides a starting point for one's journey. Those included here have one major thing in common: They all have catalogs, and they all provide mail-order services. Botánicas can be found throughout the country; all it takes is a little detective work. The easiest way is to check the business white pages for your local area. No matter the name of the business, they almost always list themselves under BOTÁNICA, followed by a Spanish or an African name. Do not look in the Yellow Pages; except in major Hispanic areas, such as Miami and New York, they do not advertise in such an expensive manner. Most are small "mom-and-pop"-type businesses and advertise their services and wares mostly by word of mouth. If no botánica can be found in your locality, the following list of businesses can be of help. Remember: Before turning to these large warehouses, try to support your own local businesses. The orishas will thank you for it!

Botánica los Guerreros
2817 Carrollton Avenue
New Orleans, LA
Phone: (504) 885-8370
This botánica is owned by a very close, dear friend of mine, a
marvelous priest of Olokun (crowned Yemayá, of course). It
carries a large array of books, candles, oils, floor washes, and
religious items used in the Lucumí faith. Yearly, the owner
produces a mail order catalog available by request. Call or write
the store for more information.

Botánica Hijos de Africa
125 Passaic Street
Passaic, NJ 07055
Phone: (973) 472-3895
Fax: (973) 472-0721
This botánica boasts that it has been serving the Passaic area for
more than six years. It specializes in religious items, natural
medicines, candles, herbs, and spiritual readings. Although I
have not had any personal dealing with this business, I have
several friends and acquaintances who have. Unanimously, they
love the shop. More information can be found about this
business on-line.

Botánica Eleguá
6043 Bissonnet
Houston, TX 77081
Phone: (713) 660-6767
Web site: www.botelegua.com
Botánica Eleguá sells everything on-line, from herbs to candles
to books and cards. Its colorful catalog may be viewed on-line.
At the time of this writing, one was not prepared specifically for
mail order; let us hope that will soon change. It does, however,
take telephone orders, giving price quotes as items are named.

Rick's Spiritual Botánica
2903 North Fifth Street
Philadelphia, PA 19133
Phone: (215) 634-7866; (215) 545-8160; (215) 546-0367
Web site: www.members.aol.com/rickspirit/index.html
Rick's Spiritual Botánica was one of the first to have a Web presence. The owner provides a wholesale catalog for bulk buyers only. A mail-order catalog (for individual buyers) indexing all his supplies and products may be ordered by phone or mail. With your first order, he does provide a free catalog; otherwise, as of this writing the cost for a catalog is two dollars.

Botánica y Rayos
6304 Hudson Avenue
West New York, NJ 07093-3016
Phone: (201) 453-0343
This botánica provides a wide range of supplies: statues, crosses, crucifixes, and African gift items. Call for a catalog and price quotes.

Botánica San Lazaro
3231 North Federal Highway
Pompano Beach, FL 33064
Phone: (954) 784-5900
Fax: The fax number is the same as the main phone number; please call before sending a fax.
Web site: www.botanicasanlaz.qpg.com
This botánica boasts more than thirty-five years of service to the community, providing a variety of spiritual supplies. Visit its Web site for more information, or call for a catalog and price quotes.

Botánica Lucumí
4748A University Way NE
Seattle, WA 98105
Phone: (206) 729-1000
Web site: www.seanet.com/~efunmoyiwa/bl.html
This is my favorite Web site and on-line botánica. It provides Ifá
and diloggún readings, all religious supplies (Lucumí and Palo),
orisha art, and too many other things to list here. Its Web site is
a "must-visit," and its customer service skills are outstanding. I
highly recommend this resource for both information and
supplies.

Botánica Shangó
240 Grand Avenue
New Haven, CT 06513
Phone: (203) 776-5501
Botánica Shangó offers mail-order supplies to individual custom-
ers and also sells wholesale supplies in bulk. Its inventory is so
large that when a Miami or New York botánica cannot obtain
needed supplies, it turns to this wholesaler. A catalog is available
free of charge; call or write to order. Unlike other botánicas
whose owners are chronically too busy to deal with their customer base, the owner of this business, Angel, is almost always
available during normal business hours. Those I know who have
done business with this store have nothing but praise for it.

Glossary

A NOTE ON THE TERMS in this glossary: Lucumí, and the original Yoruba whence it evolved, is a tonal language like Chinese. Because the Afro-Cubans had neither the time nor the chance for formal education during slavery, many of these words have no consistent spelling. While I have tried to keep my own spelling consistent throughout my work, my spellings will differ from the spellings of other authors; however, the pronunciation of the words will be similar. For any Lucumí or Spanish term that does not have an accent mark, the proper emphasis goes on the second-to-last syllable in the word. To facilitate proper pronunciation, I have included the appropriate accent for all words that vary from this pattern. Vowel sounds for all non-English words will approximate those of the Spanish language. Also note that in each glossary entry, there may be one or more words italicized; this indicates that these words can be found in the glossary as well.

Keep in mind the following points when pronouncing words.

- ♟ The *ch* sound in Spanish is used in Lucumí and Spanish words; the languages have no *sh* sound.

- The ñ character (*enye* sound) is used only in Spanish words, not Lucumí words, because it is pronounced more like the English *y* sound. So the letter *y* is used here where it applies.
- The *y* sound in Spanish has a slight edge to it so that the sounding of the letter will be similar to the English and Yoruba *j* sound. *J* is used here whenever possible.

aborisha: A *Lucumí* word that denotes one who worships the *orishas*. An *aborisha* is one who has at least the *elekes* (the necklaces of *Obatalá, Yemayá, Oshún*, and *Shangó*), although some priests and priestesses save this term for those who have gone on to receive at least the *warriors (Elegguá, Ogún, Ochosi,* and *Ósun).*

aché: This is a very dynamic, universal force. It has many meanings, among which are grace, life, fate, power, talent, and wisdom, depending on its usage. Most *santeros* will agree that life is aché and aché is life.

Adiatoto: A mythological/historical figure who lived in Africa many centuries ago; he was *Biague*'s first son.

adimú: Any type of offering that does not include *eyebale,* the sacrifice of an animal. Adimú is usually prescribed during a session with the *diloggún*.

adimú orisha: An *orisha* given who cannot be crowned on the head; a Spirit that can have no priests or priestesses in the New World. *Olokun* and the *Ibeyi* are examples of adimú orishas. The term can also refer to any orisha given outside one's *asiento.*

Aganyú: The owner of volcanoes, born from *Oroina,* the molten center of the earth. He is also the father of *Shangó.*

agó: To ask permission; permission.

ailashara: A *Lucumí* word meaning "friendship"; it is also a letter in the African system of *Obí.*

Ainá: One of the seven *Ibeyi,* or children of miraculous birth. She is the daughter of *Shangó* and his constant companion, because she is the *orisha* of all flame.

Ajé Shaluga: This *orisha* controls all aspects of luxury and wealth. Her normal guise is that of a beautiful woman, but when this spirit wants to appear as a man, she does so. Often, she will accompany *Oshún* on her travels.

akita: A *Lucumí* word meaning "victory"; it is also a letter in the African system of *Obí.*

akó: A *Lucumí* term that denotes the two phallic lobes of the seed from *Cola acuminata,* the type of kola tree from which the oracle of African *Obí* derives.

alafia: A *Lucumí* word meaning "peace" or "blessings," it also denotes a letter in the African system of *Obí* that signifies "coolness" when the response is positive. In the New World version of *Obí,* alafia brings blessings, peace, and coolness from the mighty *orisha Obatalá.* It is formed when the four pieces of coconut land with all their white rinds showing.

alafia-ejife: One of the signs of *Obí.* It is the most positive response of the *meji* castings in the family of *alafia,* and always answers yes to the client's question. It is formed when the pattern of alafia is followed by one in which show two white rinds and two black.

alafia-etawa: One of the signs of *Obí.* It is a positive response to the client's concerns. It is formed when the pattern of *alafia* is followed by one in which show three white rinds and one black.

alafia-meji: One of the signs of *Obí.* It·is a positive response to the client's concerns. It is formed when the pattern of *alafia* repeats itself.

alafia-okana: One of the signs of *Obí* in the family of alafia. It is a negative response to the client's concerns. It is formed when the pattern of *alafia* is followed by one in which show three black rinds and one white.

alafia-oyekun: One of the signs of *Obí* in the family of *alafia*. It is a negative response to the client's question, and often this pattern will attempt to address concerns with one's *egun*. It is formed when the pattern of alafia is followed by one in which show all four black rinds.

aleyo: One who is in *Santería,* yet not initiated as a priest or priestess.

amalá: A staple food of the orisha *Shangó;* it is made of okra and cornmeal.

ancestors/ancestral spirits: Also known collectively as *egun,* these may include the practitioner's familial and spiritual ancestors. Spirit guides, Congolese spirits, Native American spirits, and so on, are used in *Santería;* however, these are not egun, nor are they ancestral spirits (unless one is descended from those peoples).

ano: A *Lucumí* word meaning "illness" or "disease."

apere ti, Obí: A phrase that means, "your symbol, Obí."

arikú: A *Lucumí* word that denotes vitality, health, and immortality of the soul. It is one of the many types of *iré* that may be predicted in the *diloggún.*

Asheda: On earth, this was the first disciple of *Orúnmila*—his first priest and *Babalawo.*

asiento: The major initiation ceremony of *Santería* in which an *aleyo* becomes a *iyawó.*

Asohano: Another name for the *orisha Babaluaiye.*

avatar: Many *orishas,* such as *Obatalá, Yemayá, Oshún,* and *Elegguá,* have different avatars, or paths. These are related to their many incarnations on earth; many orishas have spent mortal lives among humans. One of the mysteries of the *asiento* is that when an *aleyo* is crowned (the *guardian orisha* is put on the head), that person becomes a *iyawó* (bride) and in some ways an avatar of the guardian orisha embodied. Only those avatars of significant religious, historical, or political importance are remembered specifically and become paths of that orisha. *Note:* Although many houses of *ocha* agree with the origins of specific avatars, the subject itself is one of considerable debate among more knowledgeable *ilé ocha*.

Ayáguna: An *avatar,* or path, of *Obatalá.* Unlike the other avatars of Obatalá, this one is young, 33 years of age. His temperament and attributes are similar to those of *Shangó.*

Ayaó: One sees this *orisha* in nature whenever a cyclone touches the earth. She is the sister of *Oyá,* very young and beautiful, who spends her free time in the woods with *Osain.*

ayé: A *Lucumí* term meaning "hardship." It is also a letter in the African system of *Obí.* When referring to the eight *ibó* used in the *diloggún,* it signifies any type of elongated saltwater seashell.

Babalawo: An initiate of *Orúnmila.* A Babalawo is always male because only men may enter *Orúnmila's* mysteries.

babalosha/babalorisha: A "father of the Spirits," a *santero* who has initiated other priests and priestesses.

Babaluaiye: This *orisha* originates not in Nigeria but in the land of Arara, an area of Africa. He is the father of smallpox and of disease and afflictions of the skin.

batea: The wooden tureen in which *Shangó's* secrets are housed.

batie sode: A Lucumí phrase meaning "removes the negativity."

Bayanmi: Another name for the brother of *Shangó,* Dada.

Biague: The first diviner to use the African system of *Obí*. The second diviner was *Adiatoto,* Biague's son. Some say that these characters are only mythological, but others believe they lived in Africa many centuries ago.

botánica: This is the Spanish term for the religious supply stores in Latin American communities that carry the items needed in the practice of *Santería*.

bóveda: An altar set up to honor and propitiate the dead, *egun*. Although it properly belongs to the practice known as *Espiritísmo,* it has been integrated into the practice of *Santería* because of the loss of the egungun cults in the New World. A bóveda can be set up to honor any spirit, even if that egun is not one of the family or ancestral spirits of the client. Certain *odu* will dictate this as *ebó*.

brujería: The Spanish term for "witchcraft" not to be confused with the type of witchcraft practiced in the New World by Wiccans or the practitioners of Palo Mayombe. It refers to any folksy charm intended to influence another for good or ill, depending on the intentions of the caster.

derecho: The ritual fee paid to an *orisha* priest or priestess for spiritual services.

Diaspora (African): The areas in the New World where the blacks uprooted from Africa were forced into slavery. Brazil, Cuba, the Caribbean, and the United States are all areas of the African Diaspora.

diloggún: The system of cowrie divination by which an *orisha* priest or priestess learns the will of the orishas. It also refers to the eighteen shells that contain the spirit, or orisha, of an initiate's shrine. The diloggún is of utmost importance to the *santero,* or practitioner of *Santería*.

divination: The act of uncovering the will of the *orishas,* the desires of *egun,* and the trends of the future. In *Santería* there are three main systems of divination: *Obí, diloggún,* and *Ifá.*

ebó: One of any number of offerings that may be made to an *orisha.*

eboda: A *Lucumí* word meaning "it is done" or "it is well." This question is often asked to close the *diloggún.*

ebó kere: A complicated series of spiritual cleansings done for a client before an *orisha.* It involves several types of offerings, each used to cleanse the supplicant of evil. It is done over a period of hours, days, weeks, or even months. The specifics of ebó kere are obtained from the *odu* of the *diloggún.*

ebó keun edun keun: One of many types of *ebó* that can be marked through *Obí.* It is a daily cleansing done before an *orisha*'s shrine.

ebó misi: One of the many types of *ebó* that can be marked through *Obí,* a daily cleansing done before an *orisha*'s shrine.

eborí: A *Lucumí* contraction of two words: *ebó* (offering) and *orí* (head). It is used to denote a blood offering to one's physical and spiritual head.

eboses: The plural of *ebó* used throughout this text. Although the Yoruba use *ebó* as both the plural and the singular, in Cuban *Santería* this has become accepted usage.

eboshure: Generally considered to be a small offering to an *orisha.*

efun: A loosely packed, powdered chalk made from crushed egg shells.

egun: One of many ancestral spirits related to the client by blood or *ocha.* The word is both singular and plural.

egungun: Denotes one who is possessed by *egun,* the ancestral spirit; in Cuba, however, it often referred to the now dead cult of egun—priests and priestesses who dealt only with the ancestral spirits and not the *orishas.*

egun onire: A *Lucumí* question which means, "Will egun give a blessing?"

ejife: The strongest response that one may receive in the oracle known as *Obí.* It consists of two white rinds and two black rinds. In a divination session, it always signifies a positive response: "Yes, the world is in balance."

Eji Ogbe: One of the sixteen *odu* in the *diloggún;* it consists of eight open mouths on the mat.

ejire: A *Lucumí* term meaning "money" or "wealth." It is also a letter used in the system of African *Obí.*

Elegguá: Also known by the names *Eshu* and *Elegbara.* He is often portrayed as fate, a young child, and an old man. Elegguá is the messenger of all the *orishas,* and the first and last to be honored in every ceremony performed. Without his goodwill, nothing in the religion *Santería* may be done. In *Ifá* it is said that there are 256 paths of *Elegguá,* one for each *odu.* Each of these paths in known as Eshu and has its own specific name, such as *Eshu Aye, Eshu Bi,* or *Eshu Laroye.* In *ocha,* there are 101 paths of *Elegguá* (each also known as Eshu). In many *ilé ocha,* when an initiate receives the *warriors* he is told the name of Eshu that his Elegguá enshrines.

elekes: The beaded necklaces given to both *aleyos* and *santeros.* The bead colors denote not only the *orisha* to whom they are consecrated, but also the path of that orisha. In the initiation of the elekes, an aleyo will generally receive four elekes —*Obatalá, Yemayá, Oshún,* and *Shangó*—unless the *diloggún* specifies otherwise. Sometimes the eleke of *Elegguá* is also given.

entrada: Twenty-one days after an *aleyo* brings home the *warriors,* the ritual of entrada must be done. Behind the front door of the home, two roosters and two pigeons are fed to *Elegguá, Ogún, Ochosi,* and *Ósun.* One week after that, they are given a basket of cool fruits. This is a welcoming, a housewarming party for these four *orishas.* It seats them firmly in the aleyo's life and home.

epó: A thick, viscous red palm oil used for cooking in Africa, and also as an *adimú* offering for certain *orishas: Elegguá, Ogún,* and *Ochosi* often take red palm oil on their sacred stones.

Eshu, Esu: Alternate names for the orisha commonly known as *Elegguá.* While *Ifá* lists one Eshu for each of the 256 *odu, ocha* has only 101 paths of Eshu. Some examples of Eshu that are shared by both Ifá and ocha are *Eshu Aye, Eshu Laroye,* and *Eshu Bi.*

Eshu Ayé: This *avatar* of *Elegguá* is said to walk on the shoreline where waves lap at the sand. This *Eshu* works closely with the *orisha Olokun.*

Eshu Bi: This *avatar* of *Elegguá* is both a young child and an old man. He is forceful and stern. It is said that this *Eshu* walks with the first two *Ibeyi,* the twins, who were born of *Shangó* and *Oshún.* He is the protector of twins, and also of small children.

Eshu Eshun Irirke: This *avatar* of *Elegguá* works closely with *Osain* and lives in the forest with that *orisha.* This *Eshu* is very rare, and is referred to in only one *odu* of the *diloggún,* Ogbe Ejila (8–12).

Eshu Laroye: This *avatar* of *Elegguá* works closely with *Oshún* and is her constant companion. He is often referred to as the "little talkative one." He is one of *Elegguá's* most important and popular paths, being the one addressed and refreshed before any invocation or prayer to the *orishas.*

Espiritísmo: A Spanish term describing the collective mediumistic practices, or Spiritualism, begun by Allan Kardec. In *Santería,* these practices are among the many used to make up for the loss of the *egungun* cults in the New World.

espiritista: A Spanish term denoting the practitioner of *Espiritísmo,* a medium. It is used for both male and female practitioners.

etawa: A *Lucumí* contraction that means "three have come"; it refers to the opening of the letter in *Obí* in which three white sides and one black are showing.

etawa-alafia: One of the patterns that exist in *Obí's* family of *etawa.* It is formed when the pattern known as etawa is followed by one of all white rinds. It is positive, answering yes to the client's concerns.

etawa-ejife: One of the patterns that exist in *Obí's* family of *etawa.* It is formed when the pattern known as etawa is followed by one of two white rinds and two black. It is the most positive answer, and always answers yes to the client's concerns.

etawa-meji: One of the patterns that exist in *Obí's* family of *etawa.* It is formed when the pattern known as etawa is followed by itself. It is not the most positive response, but can be taken as a yes to the client's question.

etawa-okana: One of the patterns that exist in *Obí's* family of *etawa.* It is formed when the pattern known as etawa is followed by one of three dark rinds and one white rind. It is a negative response, and answers no to the client's original question.

etawa-oyekun: One of the patterns that exist in *Obí's* family of *etawa.* It is formed when the pattern known as etawa is followed by one of all black rinds. It is the most negative response. It may also bring up issues with *egun* that must be resolved before the session can be closed.

ewe: A *Lucumí* word for "herb"; it denotes any of those plants, roots, or trees that are used in the making of herbal baths, mixtures, medicines, or *omiero*.

eyebale: An offering that includes the sacrifice of an animal.

foribale: One of the two methods of salutation to an elder or an *orisha;* the form of salutation depends on whether the guardian *orisha* is male or female.

funfún: White, cool.

godparents: In *Santería,* the godparents are one's sponsors in the religion, the priests or priestesses who will give the initiations of the *elekes, warriors,* and *asiento.* They are the aspirant's spiritual guides in both life and religion, and are consulted on all matters of spiritual importance.

gofio: Roasted flour or cornmeal.

guardian orisha: The *orisha* who claims an *aleyo,* guiding him or her to the ritual of *asiento.* Once *ocha* is made (initiation given), the aleyo becomes a *iyawó* (bride) of the guardian orisha, and after a year becomes a *santero* (priest) or *santera* (priestess) in *Santería.*

Ibeyi: The divine children of *Shangó* and *Oshún.* There are seven Ibeyi, also known as children of miraculous birth. The first two Ibeyi are twins whom *Oshún* gave to her sister *Yemayá* to raise. It has become common usage in *Santería* for practitioners to refer to these first two children as "the Ibeyi." They are the patrons of twins and of the mothers of twins.

Ideu: The third *Ibeyi,* a child of *Oshún.* It is a male, and yet it is always accompanied by a doll dressed as a small girl.

Ifá: The original oracle of the *Yoruba* on which both the African and Afro-Cuban forms of *diloggún* (cowrie shell) divination are based. It is a system that includes 256 *odu,* revealed by *Orúnmila* to his disciples *Asheda* and *Akoda* (the first *Babalawos*). Only the priests of *Orúnmila,* the Babalawos, may read Ifá.

igboro larishe: A *Lucumí* question that means, "will an initiate have the remedy?"

Ikú: The *Lucumí* personification of death.

Ilé Ifé: In *Yoruba* mythology, the holy city that was built first in the empire. It was founded by *Obatalá* himself, and it is the cradle from which our religion *Santería* eventually evolved.

ile ocha: This is a *Lucumí* term that refers to the spiritual house of *ocha* headed by a specific priest or priestess.

Ilé Ilú: In Lucumí mythology, the city in which Biague lived in Africa (in the area now known as Nigeria). It is the town in which Obí divination was first used.

Ilé Olófin: For those *santeros* who retain their Catholic identity, this is the Catholic Church; for those whose beliefs are pure *Lucumí,* this term refers to all of nature, the true home of God.

Inle: He is envisioned as a beautiful androgynous youth, the patron of homosexuals and fishermen. At one time he was a mortal, but *Yemayá* was so taken by his beauty that she made him immortal and stole away Inle to the bottom of the sea. There she tired of him, yet he learned all of his lover's secrets. *Yemayá* removed his speech by cutting out his tongue, and then she set him free to walk among the rest of the *orishas*. To this day, Inle will speak only through her. He is also seen as the great physician, the one who can cure any illness with his extensive knowledge of the medicinal uses of all *ewe* in the forest.

Irawo: A *Lucumí* word that means star; it is also the name of a town in which Orisha Oko ruled while living on earth as a mortal.

iré: Any type of good fortune that can befall the client as he sits for a session with the *diloggún*.

Irunmole: The first *orisha* born in heaven from *Olódumare* and *odu*.

Itá: A major divination ceremony given either to a *iyawó* after the *asiento* or to a priest or priestess who has fed an orisha a four-legged animal as *ebó*. The information, eboses, and prohibitions prescribed during an itá are followed by an initiate for life.

iyala: A Yoruba word meaning "health"; it is also one of the letters found in the African system of *Obí*.

iyalocha: A *santera*, or priestess of *Santería*, who has initiated at least one other person into the mysteries.

iyawó: A *Lucumí* term for the initiate of an *orisha*. It literally means "bride," no matter the initiate's sex. For at least a year after the *asiento*, the rest of the initiates in the house will refer to this person by this term.

Jakuta: Once a powerful *orisha* in the *Yoruba* pantheon, the "stone thrower" and wielder of the lightning bolt. With the rise of the followers of *Shangó*, however, the cult of Jakuta died and was replaced by Shangó's.

jícara: A dried gourd that is cut open to resemble a bowl. It is used to give offerings and to pour libations to the *orishas*.

jutía: An African bush rat, a large rodent. It is a staple offering for many of the *warrior orishas* such as *Elegguá, Ogún,* and *Ochosi*.

Kaindé: The second *Ibeyi* born of *Oshún* and *Shangó*; this Ibeyi is female, and her name means "the final to be born."

kaure: One of the many types of *ebó* that can be marked through *Obí*; it is a series of prayers offered to the *orishas* on a daily basis.

kawo kabiosile: A praise given to *Shangó*. It refers to the fact that the king (Shangó) did not hang (kill himself by suicide). He ascended before death to become an *orisha*.

kinkanmaché: This *Lucumí* word is a contraction that asks for protection, blessings, and the good things in life.

koborí eledá: An *ebó*, usually a *rogación,* done to one's *orí*. It can involve any type of offering or cleansing that does not include animal sacrifice.

kola nut *(Cola acuminata):* A tropical species of tree prolific in Africa but scarce in the New World. It is the tree that provides the seed from which the *Yoruba* derive their own system of *Obí* divination.

larishe: One of the hundreds of remedies that any one *odu* can prescribe to overcome *osogbo* and bring *iré* to the client sitting for a session with the *diloggún.*

lavado: Spanish for "washed." All *orishas* must be washed and born in *omiero.* When one's orisha is received outside the ritual of *asiento,* it is known as *santo lavado.*

lavatorio: The birthing of an *orisha* in which the *otanes* (shells) and implements of an initiate's new orisha are washed in *omiero* and are born from a godparent's orisha. See also *Osain.*

Lazareros: *Aborishas* or initiates who have received the initiation of the *orisha Babaluaiye.*

Lucumí: A contraction of various *Yoruba* words, meaning "my friend." The Lucumí are the physical, and now spiritual, descendants of the black Yoruba slaves in Cuba. This word also refers to the corruption of the native Yoruba tongue, which is now used in *Santería.*

Maferefún: Praise be to; all power be to.

mandala: A magical image or symbol. In the system of *Obí*, it refers to the patterns that can fall when the coconuts are cast before an *orisha*.

Meji: Twin, double.

misa : Sometimes called a seance, this is a ritual of *Espiritísmo* done to honor the dead. It involves prayers, offerings, and medium possessions.

modupue: A *Lucumí* term meaning "I thank you."

mojuba: A prayer recited to give homage to an *orisha* or *egun*.

mojubando: The act of reciting a prayer giving homage to an *orisha*.

mojubar: The act of giving praise or homage to an *orisha* or *egun*.

mulatto: A Spanish word denoting a person who has one parent of Caucasian heritage and one of African-American heritage.

Naná Burukú: In some mythologies, this *orisha* was born from *Yembo* when she ascended by her own *aché* to the palace of *Olódumare;* historically, she comes from the land of Arara in Africa and is not *Yoruba*. She was later syncretized into the *Santería* pantheon during the time of the *cabildos* (secret clubs) in Cuba. She is the mother of *Nanumé* and *Babaluaiye*.

Nanumé: A very old and female *avatar* of *Babaluaiye*. So dissociated from him is she that many consider her to be not only an aspect of this *orisha*, but his sister and a separate entity as well (similar to the relationship between *Yemayá* and *Yembo*). She is the daughter of *Naná Burukú,* and is said by elder *santeros* to be the moon in the night sky.

ñame: A type of yam, a root used frequently in Latin American cuisine.

Oba: An *orisha* considered to be *Shangó's* only official wife; she is but one among three of his lovers. The other two were *Oshún* and *Oyá.*

Obara Osá: One of the 256 patterns of the *diloggún,* a more extensive oracle used by the *Lucumí* faith. Obara Osá contains the story of *Obí's* fall from grace.

Obatalá: An *orisha* considered to be the king of all the orishas and the creator of humans.

Obí: The man who became *orisha* and then fell from grace because of his own pride, becoming the coconut used in divination. Despite this, Obí is still an orisha and is treated with respect in *Santería.*

ocha: A shortened form of the word *orisha;* it is also used at times to denote *Santería.*

Ochanlá: One of *Obatalá's* eldest *avatars* on earth.

Ochosi: An *orisha;* one of the *warriors* and said to be the patron of the hunt.

Ochúmaré: An androgynous *orisha* born from *Naná Burukú.* S/he is the rainbow, the crown of *Yemayá.* Some say this is the patron spirit of gays, lesbians, and bisexuals. Half the year this *orisha* lives deep in the river and never touches dry earth; during the other half, she lives on earth and never touches water.

Odi: One of the sixteen letters of the *diloggún;* also, one of the ten signs of African *Obí.*

Odua: An elder *avatar* of *Obatalá.* Many believe this path to be a female avatar of the *orisha.*

Oduduwa: The founder of the *Yoruba* empire. He is also a warrior *orisha.*

Ogún: One of the many *orishas* in the *Lucumí* pantheon. He is the spirit of iron and controls its vast stores beneath the earth.

Ojigbona: The assistant to one's godparent; also spelled *yubonna*.

okana: One of many patterns that may appear before an *orisha* when *Obí* is cast. It consists of three black rinds and one white. It is usually negative, but can give a positive response in some circumstances.

okana-alafia: One of the more positive responses in the family of *okana*. It is formed when okana is followed by a pattern of all white rinds.

okana-ejife: The most positive response in the family of *okana*. It is formed when *okana* is followed by a pattern of two white and two black rinds.

okana-etawa: One of the more positive responses in the family of *okana*. It is formed when okana is followed by a pattern of three white rinds and one black.

okana-meji: One of the more negative responses in the family of *okana*. It is formed when okana is followed by a pattern of three black rinds and one white. It has doubled itself, and thus is called a *meji,* a twin.

okana-oyekun: The most negative response in the family of *okana*, will always mean no to the client's concern; it can also flag issues with one's *egun*. It is formed when okana is followed by a pattern of all black rinds.

Oké: Referred to as *Orisha Oké,* he is the spirit of the mountain, the first point of land that rose from *Olokun*'s watery domain. Orisha Oké is where *Obatalá* came to earth; it is his foundation and strength, and Oké acts as his messenger between heaven and earth.

Olocha: A *Lucumí* contraction signifying one who has *ocha* done; an initiate of *Santería*.

Olódumare: A *Yoruba* contraction meaning "owner of the womb"; this is the supreme deity of the Yoruba and the *Lucumí*.

Olófin: It is said among the *Lucumí* that Olófin is "god on earth." He is the eldest *avatar* of *Obatalá*, and can be received only by the priesthood of *Orúnmila*, the *Babalawos*.

Olokun: The androgynous *orisha* who rules and owns the deepest parts of the sea.

Olorún: A *Lucumí* contraction of two words—*olo*, "owner", and *orún*, "the sun"—it means "owner of the sun." It is a name for God, his symbol being the sun in the daytime sky.

Olosa: One of the minor orishas, the spirit of the lagoon.

Oluwo: Lord of awós, a *Babalawo* who made ocha before making *Ifá*.

omiero: Any of a number of herbal waters made by initiates of *Santería;* it is used in bathing the *Iyawó* and giving birth to the *orishas*.

omo: Child.

onire: A *Lucumí* contraction meaning "[to give a blessing] to clear a sign."

Opá ikú: Staff of the dead.

Opele: A *Babalawo's* divining chain.

orí: A *Yoruba* word meaning "head/consciousness"; it is used to refer to the spiritual head of the client.

orisha: A *Yoruba* contraction meaning "select head"; it denotes any of the myriad spirits in the pantheon of *Santería* that are an extension of *Olódumare's aché*.

orisha Oko: The *orisha* who controls the fecundity of the earth. He has two forms: During the day he is envisioned as a handsome black male; at night he becomes a terrifying presence in the darkness. Traditionally, this orisha lives in the *santero's* home for the six months that the fields lie fallow, then he goes outdoors with the beginning of the planting season (our house does this on the spring equinox and takes him back inside on the autumn equinox).

Oroina: Lives at the center of the earth; she is its molten core. She gave birth to the *orisha Aganyú.*

orún: The Lucumí word for the sun.

Orúnla: The *orisha* of the diviners, the *Babalawos.* Only men are called to his priesthood. He is also known as *Orúnmila.*

Orúnmila: Another name for *Orúnla.*

Osain: One of the most mysterious *orishas,* Osain was created after creation. He sprang forth from the earth at the moment the first green thing began to grow. He is the lord of *aché* on earth, knowing all the secrets of the *ewe.* Without Osain, none of the orishas can work their magic, nor can their children be initiated, nor can the orishas be born on earth. He will live until the last green thing on this planet perishes. Anyone born with either six fingers or six toes is said to be an *Osainista* from birth.

osainista: A priest or priestess of the orisha *Osain.* An osainista is either claimed by him in the *diloggún* or claimed by birth (his mark being six fingers or toes).

Oshún: The *orisha* bringing love, sweetness, money, prosperity, fertility, conception, and all the things that make life worth living. She is the sister of *Yemayá* and one of *Shangó's* three wives.

osogbo: Any of the evils that may be predicted for a client through the oracle known as *diloggún.*

Ósun: Some in the New World consider Ósun a minor *orisha;* however, there are many types of Ósuns that can be given in different initiations—that of the *warriors, Babaluaiye, Naná Burukú,* and *Inle.* Ósun is an orisha in one sense, the Spirit that guards the *orí* of the client from danger. Yet more properly, Ósun is the herbal staff of *Osain* that is packed with herbs and secrets specific to the orisha given to an adherent.

otá/otanes: The sacred stones that house the spirit of an *orisha* to whom they are consecrated. Their number and color will depend on the orisha embodied.

Otín: An *orisha* whose sole purpose is to serve *Yemayá.*

Owani Ofún: One of the 256 patterns found in the more extensive oracle known as the *diloggún;* it is the sign that speaks of *Biague* and *Adiatoto,* the first diviners with *Obí.*

Oyá: This female *orisha* is the patron of the "fire in the sky," or lightning that does not touch the earth. She is the gatekeeper to the cemetery, *Shangó's* partner in battle, and the lady of the marketplace. Some also see her in the action of the tornado. This is Shangó's third wife, and his favorite even over *Oshún.*

oyekun: One of the patterns found in *Obí* that may fall when the coconuts are cast before the *orishas.* It always answers no to the client's question. This pattern may also flag issues with one's *egun.* It is formed when all black rinds are displayed before the orisha questioned.

Oyó: A city in Nigeria from which many *orisha* priest/esses were forced into slavery. There are two types of Oyó referenced in *Santería.* The first is "Old Oyó," the city from which the slaves were forcefully taken. Old Oyó is spread throughout the *African Diaspora,* and is the Oyó from which many of our traditions grew. Old Oyó is no longer a place one may visit; it is found in the faces and souls of those who practice Santería. New Oyó is the city that remained in the motherland and evolved new sets of customs that are not observed in the New World's version of orisha worship. In the Cuban rites of Santería, it is the customs of Old Oyó that are observed in ritual.

pañuelo: A decorative cloth cover draped over the tureen of an *orisha.*

patakís: The many sacred stories and legends found in the *diloggún;* some of these are about the *orishas,* while others are about the actions of historical/mythological humans who lived and died in both African and Cuba.

rogación: A cleansing of the head, the client's *orí.* It involves grated coconut as the main ingredient and a series of prayers to strengthen and support the head. The specifics of each rogación are given in each *odu* of the *diloggún.*

Santería: The name of *orisha* worship as it developed in Cuba; the English translation from the Spanish means "worship of the saints." It was given this name because of the syncretizing of the Catholic saints and the orishas of the *Yoruba.*

santero/santera: A priest/priestess of *Santería.*

sarayeye: One of the many types of *ebó* that can be marked with *Obí.* It is a cleansing, and sometimes might involve the use of an animal. If sarayeye is marked with an animal, however, that animal is set free after the cleansing is complete. If a sacrifice is called for, the oracle will mark *eyebale* as the ebó needed to help the client evolve.

Shangó: An *orisha* who once lived on earth as a mortal; he was the fourth king of *Oyó,* and tried to punish himself for his own crimes by hanging. The prior force of his good deeds, however, would not let the hanging be completed; before his death he ascended to become an orisha.

sopera: A Spanish word for "tureen"; it denotes the bowls where the *otanes* and implements of the *orishas* are kept.

spiritism: The practice of working with the spirits of the dead. It was begun in France by Allan Kardec. Spiritism takes the place of the *egungun* cults that were lost in Cuba during the slave trade.

Taewó: The first *Ibeyi* born of *Oshún* and *Shangó*. This child is male, and his name means "first to taste life."

tambor: The sacred festival of an *orisha* in which drums are played and the mounts are possessed by their orishas.

thunderstone: The dark black, smooth, glassy stones in which *Shangó* is said to reside. They are virtually indestructible, believed to have been formed wherever lightning has touched the earth.

warriors: The three *orishas* who are received together in one initiation: *Elegguá, Ogún,* and *Ósun*. A simulacrum of *Ochosi* is received with Ogún in the form of an iron crossbow.

Yemayá: Born when *Olokun* was chained to the bottom of the ocean by *Obatalá*, Yemayá arose to become mother to the world and to the orishas. She is the patron of motherhood and of the fresh waters of the world.

Yembo: There is confusion over exactly who this female *orisha* is. Some say she is an elder path of *Obatalá*. Because she was once the wife of Obatalá, however, our house believes her to be an ancestral *Yemayá*. She is mother of the orishas and gave birth to all the waters of the world. *Naná Burukú* was born after Yembo was raped by *Ogún*. Yembo ascended to *Olódumare's* palace by her own grief and *aché*, creating the moon and Naná Burukú to watch over women and punish those who commit crimes against them.

Yewá/Yeguá: A very young, gorgeous *orisha*, yet she is the most chaste of them all, a virgin. She demands no less of her priestesses (men never may be initiated to her mysteries). Many know her as the devourer of the dead; she decomposes the bodies that lie in the earth's grasp.

yeyé: Mother.

Yoruba: The native Africans who originally settled in the southwestern parts of the area known today as Nigeria. Their deities, the *orishas,* form the basis for the religion *Santería.* The word *Yoruba* also denotes the language shared by these peoples, the native tongue that mixed with Cuban Spanish to become *Lucumí.*

yubonna: A *Lucumí* title for the priest or priestess who assists one's godparent in the rituals of the *elekes, warriors,* and *asiento.* See also, *ojigbona.*

Suggested Reading

FOR THOSE WHO DESIRE more general information about Santería and its basic beliefs, the following books are highly recommended.

Canizares, Raul. *Walking with the Night.* Rochester, Vt.: Destiny Books, 1993.
This book is a wonderful testament to the power of Santería from a man who not only was raised in the religion, but was also initiated at a very young age. It is filled with anecdotes and personal stories that illustrate the intervention of the orishas in his life. Inspirational, it is a must-read for those involved in all levels of the religion.

Flores, Ysamur. *Santería Garments and Altars.* Jackson, Miss.: University Press of Mississippi, 1994.
This book was written in conjunction with Peña and Roberto J. Evenchuk. It is an exceptional overview of the faith's religious elements. Unlike other books written today that promise to teach the religion by a series of "how-tos" that read like an esoteric cookbook, this volume instructs the reader about the

faith and its orishas by depicting various coronation gowns and suits, along with a variety of celebration and anniversary altars for the orishas. It gives a splendid feel for the religion and its celebrations. It is a hardcover book filled with color plates and photographs, and although it is costly and a bit hard to find, it is well worth the reader's investment in time and money.

González-Wippler, Migene. *Introduction to Seashell Divination.* Plainview, N.Y.: Original Publications, 1992.

———*Legends of Santería.* St. Paul, Minn.: Lewellyn Publications, 1994.

———*Powers of the Orishas.* Plainview, N.Y.: Original Publications, 1992.

———*Rituals and Spells of Santería.* New York: Original Publications, 1984.

———*Santería: African Magic in Latin America.* New York: Original Publications,1973.

———*The Santería Experience.* St. Paul, Minn.: Lewellyn Publications, 1994.

——— *Santería, the Religion.* St. Paul, Minn.: Lewellyn Publications, 1994.
Although many have criticized her for popularizing the magical side of Santería while downplaying the religious elements, González-Wippler has corrected much of this in the later editions of her work, especially those published by Llewellyn Publications. Were it not for her writings, many of those now in the religion never would have found Santería.

Neimark, Philip John. *The Sacred Ifá Oracle.* New York: HarperCollins, 1995.

————*The Way of the Orisa.* New York: HarperCollins,: 1993.
The descriptions of the orishas (Neimark spells them *Orisa)* and
the attributes are among the best I have read; however, I cannot
help but disagree with his conception of Yemayá/Olokun as
being one and the same orisha. Although I am an initiate of
Santería, I have met a few African priests in my lifetime and
none of them agrees with his conception of "how things are
done in Africa." Yet this book, as a whole, is a wonderful introduction to the orishas as seen from the eyes of a newly initiated
Babalawo.

For those who wish to read additional material dealing with
the African faith as it is practiced in Nigeria or the African forms
of divination, the following books are recommended.

Bascom, William R. *Ifá Divination.* Bloomington, Ind.: Indiana
University Press, 1969.

————*Shangó in the New World.* Austin, Tex.: University of Texas
at Austin,1972.

————*Sixteen Cowries.* Bloomington, Ind.: Indiana University
Press, 1970.
William Bascom is the American authority on African spirituality.
Although none of his books provides the instructional material
needed to work any of the oracles, his writings are filled with
scholarly information about the African traditions. His two books
on the oracles, *Sixteen Cowries* and *Ifá Divination,* are filled with a
wealth of patakís for each odu, and our diviners are continually
turning to these volumes as a source of information and clarifica-
tion.

Fatunmbi, Awó Fa'Lokun. *Awó: Ifá and the Theology of Orisha
Divination.* New York: Original Publications, 1992.
Although this book is often criticized by orisha priests and
priestesses for its innovations of the casting of four cowries in
place of four coconut rinds to read the oracle Obí, it is also

praised for its detailed metaphysics. A book that brings controversy also brings much thought—I recommend it for its provocative content.

Idowu, E. Bolaji. *Olódumare: God in Yoruba Belief*. New York: Original Publications, 1995.
This is the best book available about the supreme deity of Yoruba belief; it also sheds light on the original practices that spawned the religion we now practice. It is essential reading for those either in the faith or about to enter it.

INDEX